ADDICT at 10

How I Overcame Addiction,
Poverty, and Homelessness to
Become a Millionaire by 35

DEREK STEELE

Synergy Books

Addict at Ten: How I Overcame Addiction, Poverty, and
Homelessness to Become a Millionaire by 35
Published by Synergy Books
P.O. Box 80107
Austin, TX 78758

For more information about our books, please write us, e-mail us at
info@synergybooks.net, or visit our web site at www.synergybooks.net.

Publisher's Cataloging-in-Publication
(Provided by Quality Books, Inc.)

Steele, Derek.
    Addict at ten : how I overcame addiction, poverty,
and homelessness to become a millionaire by 35 / Derek
Steele.
        p. cm.
    LCCN 2009936109
    ISBN-13: 978-0-9840760-9-3
    ISBN-10: 0-9840760-9-3

    1. Steele, Derek. 2. Recovering addicts--Biography.
3. Millionaires--Biography. 4. Addicts--Biography.
5. Homeless persons--Biography. 6. Recovering addicts'
writings, American. I. Title.

HV5805.S74A3 2010   362.29'092
                             QBI09-600158

This book is written with the intent of being as accurate as possible. It
is based upon how the author remembers events and experiences.

10 9 8 7 6 5 4 3 2 1

FOREWORD

Our pasts have no power over our future when we have God to guide the way. This principle is the basis of Christian-based counseling, and is the message of this heart-wrenching story of extraordinary personal transformation written by Derek Steele. In today's busy, spiritually starved society, there are people of all ages who find themselves lost, hopeless, addicted, or obsessed, and without a personal relationship with God. Often they have sought to find a better way but have failed miserably. Each day we meet them. They are our family, friends, and coworkers. They are the strangers in the grocery store. Perhaps even you are one of them.

In *Addict at Ten*, Derek Steele relates his own turbulent voyage from hopelessness to faith, and from despair to awe-inspiring promise, sharing with us the principles and disciplines he used to strengthen his faith in God and skyrocket himself to personal success and achievement. His journey is an inspiration to anyone seeking to lead a better life, whether they now find themselves lost in the pit of despair that addiction can bring, or are merely seeking guidance on how to strengthen their relationships with God and family.

I recommend that you read this book carefully, and educate yourself on the disciplines and tools that Derek employed to triumph over adversity when all odds were against him. Then pray, roll your sleeves up, and put those principles to work to forge a better future. Share them with your friends, family, and others in need. As Derek came to understand, there is no luck in this life—God always has a plan for us. No matter what obstacles you face from your past, your future can be yours with God's help and your own personal dedication to change. God bless, and enjoy.

—Tim Clinton, EdD, President of the American Association of Christian Counselors

ACKNOWLEDGMENTS

First and foremost, I would like to thank God for all of the grace and gifts that He has given me throughout my life. I also would not be the man I am today if it weren't for my amazing wife, Becky, and our two beautiful children. Becky has been my rock since we began dating. My sponsor Scott B. has also been my rock in sobriety, and I can't say enough thanks to him for always being there when I needed him. I would also like to thank my family for supporting me while I wrote this book, and last but not least, I would like to thank all of the men and women in twelve step programs who have supported me over the years.

PROLOGUE

The sun pouring in the window woke me up. It was already stiflingly warm, both inside and outside of my truck, and too bright to sleep anymore. My head was pounding, and I knew the sunlight was not going to help my hangover at all. I sat up slowly and opened the window, taking a few deep breaths, but since the air was so humid, it didn't bring any relief. I yawned and stretched, cursing as I bumped my hand on the roof of the truck. Might as well get moving.

I started my truck, flipped on the air conditioner, and glanced at the clock. I had a lot of time to kill but nothing in the world to do. Since it was past seven in the morning, I decided to drive to the nearest 7-Eleven and get my day started with a six-pack of Bud. After stopping at the convenience store, I drove to an empty parking lot, lit up a joint, and had a few beers, thinking about the crucial deal I was going to make that night.

It was risky; I knew that. But I was up against the wall. I'd been busted a couple of months before for a hot check scam that

I'd only been nominally involved in. A guy I knew was doing a scam with hot checks, and he came by one day and offered me a thousand dollars' worth of ecstasy in exchange for my driver's license. He was going to use it to go out and cash some forged checks. For my protection, I was supposed to go report my license lost or stolen at the DPS office the next day, no problem. Unfortunately, that never happened because, as usual, I got really wasted and forgot all about it. About six weeks later, I went to get a new license at DPS, and they took me to jail for the hot check scam. Luckily, after several days in hell, also known as Harris County Jail, I was released on bail.

My conviction for the check scam had recently come through; I'd been offered either two years in prison or five years' deferred adjudication. The conditions of my probation included community service and monthly drug tests, polygraphs, and reports to my parole officer. I didn't want to go to prison, so I took the deferred adjudication. It was a pretty reasonable deal, but in my heart I knew I'd never pass the drug tests—or the polygraphs either, for that matter. If I failed, the two years would be off the table and I would get the full five years in prison.

That's why I had worked out this one last deal. I had decided the only way out of this mess was to leave the country, and I needed cash to make that happen. Once I made up my mind to leave, the rest was surprisingly easy. I had already skipped out on my first drug test and a meeting with my parole officer; there had just been no point in going. This guy named Manuel, who I was doing the deal with, had convinced a dealer he knew to front us a twenty-five-pound bale of pot, which would finance the chemicals I needed to make about a hundred thousand tablets of ecstasy. There was a house in El

Campo, south of Houston, in which I could set up a lab, and a chemist in Dallas who would help me manufacture the pills. If I sold the ecstasy tablets for eight dollars each, then even after splitting the money three ways, I figured I could move to Mexico or Jamaica. It wasn't a perfect plan, but I didn't have a lot of options anymore. I'd been living in my truck for a couple of months and the misery of being homeless was more than I could stand. The thought of going to prison for five years scared me to death.

I wasn't particularly worried about that night's meeting. Getting the bale this far had been the hard part. I met Manuel and his dealer at a pay phone, and we made the exchange and left in separate cars. The bale, wrapped in garbage bags, lay on the floorboard of my truck. Within a minute after the swap, a cop blew around me and stopped Manuel and his dealer. I drove right on by. There was nothing in his car they could bust him for. It was a close call that could have cost me the five years I was already facing and probably another twenty for all the pot in my truck. I was lucky.

I drove to Manuel's house and parked on the street. I'd been sleeping in my truck in front of his house for a while. He lived with his parents and sisters, so I couldn't stay with him. For one thing, they didn't have room; for another, they didn't like me. Manuel had only recently gotten out of prison for assault and possession, so I was the last person they wanted him associating with. By nine o'clock, his parents had left for work, so I went inside to take a shower. Then Manuel and I sat around drinking and getting high for most of the day.

Around dusk, I drove to a McDonald's and decided to go in to get dinner and stretch my legs. I covered the bale carefully with some clothes and parked up front where I could see if anybody messed with my truck; everything I owned was in that truck, not to mention my whole future. I ordered a Big Mac and ignored the expression on the girl's face. I knew I looked like crap—long, unkempt hair, sunken cheeks, bloodshot eyes. I was used to it. As I ate, I made plans for my share of the money, trying to figure out exactly how far it would go in pesos.

Finally, it was time. I headed downtown toward the warehouse. I parked in back and sat there for a minute, thinking about what was going to happen next, wondering where I'd be next week, and what my life would be like a year from now. Then I shook my head, got out of the car, and carried in the bale of pot. Manuel was already there when I walked in; I nodded at him and set the bale down on a worktable against the wall. We were in an old, empty warehouse in a seedy part of town, and I was worried that the guys bringing the chemicals might rip us off. Manuel and I could end up getting shot if this deal went south for some reason. Within a few minutes, we heard the creaking groan of the ill-fitting metal door, which signaled the arrival of the guys with the chemicals we needed.

"You got it?" one of them said.

"Yep," I replied. "You?"

"Yep. Here it is."

I looked at the cases of bottles and saw at a glance that they'd brought the wrong stuff. I cursed, fluidly and obscenely.

"This is supposed to be MDP."

"Yeah," one of the guys said, gesturing to the bottles. "So?"

"So, it's MEK! This doesn't do me any damn good!"

"Well, we can get the right stuff, man. We just need some time."

I looked at the guy in disbelief. I could feel my life falling down around me. My knees shook with the gravity of the situation, and I leaned over and rested my hands on them. There wasn't time to fix this, and I knew I was screwed. I was out of money, I had no place to live, the police would be issuing a warrant for my arrest any day now, and I knew these guys were lying about being able to get the right chemicals.

In that moment, something profound happened. I suddenly realized with absolute clarity and utter certainty who and what I was—a drug addict, a liar, a thief, and a criminal. A complete and total loser. That's what I'd become. I couldn't even remember the little boy I had once been. I hated my life, I hated myself, and I knew I needed help. It was almost as if I were looking at myself from an outsider's perspective. I could finally see myself for who and what I really was. I stood there, trembling, and I thought about what this would mean. It would mean jail, and it would mean getting clean—I didn't know which would be harder. It would mean everyone in my life who didn't already know what I was would find out. The realization of what my life had become hit me with a pain so deep it was physical. My ears rang, and my breaths came in short, painful gasps. Memories, hopes, and fears rushed through my brain, leaving me dizzy and disoriented. What had happened to me, and why had I done this to myself? I didn't know how to fix my life. I didn't know how to be anything other than an addict. For years, I had been lying to myself about who and what I was. My perception of myself and the life I had been living had been warped to the point where I thought my behavior was normal. However, in this one moment of perfect clarity, I finally saw the reality of what my life had become, and it was the scariest and most depressing thing I had ever experienced.

I heard Manuel talking to me, asking me something, and his voice sounded far away. I stood up straight.

"I'm out of here, guys," I said. "Lose my number."

I turned and walked out without waiting for a response.

PART 1

CHAPTER 1

While growing up, my sister and I were alone a lot. My dad worked for a furniture company and had to travel all the time, and my mom was a bartender, so their hours were all over the place. They met in Denver in 1972, and had me soon after—accidentally, as my dad frequently chose to remind me. You could say it was a shotgun wedding, but without the indignant father of the bride.

My parents were attractive, sociable people. My dad was tall, lean, and blue-eyed, my mom thin and tan, and both of them were very stylish—at least as stylish as anyone was in the seventies. They each had permed hair teased into a big 'fro, and my dad had a large mustache. With their matching hairstyles and bell-bottoms, they looked like the perfect couple. My sister Dawn, the product of my mom's first marriage, was a cute little freckle-faced redhead. I had my share of freckles, too, but with much different coloring from Dawn's, with my blond hair and blue eyes.

3

Dawn was five years older than me, so she always considered me "her baby" and took great pride in taking care of me. I was an extremely sick baby, and my constant health problems were a strain on my already resistant father. As an infant, I contracted salmonella from our water and almost died. Striking me at such a young age, this caused really high fevers, which did something to my brain that affected my ability to feel pain. I couldn't feel any pain until I was about ten years old, which made me pretty hard to discipline. Time-out was not a popular parenting concept in the mid-seventies, and corporal punishment had little impact on me. In fact, once, when I was three or four, my grandmother spanked me for misbehaving; irritated but undeterred, I threw myself to the floor and bit her on the ankle.

When I was three, we moved from Colorado to Katy, Texas, a suburb of Houston. My dad managed a furniture store and my mom quit bartending and moved into retail, landing a commissioned sales job downtown. She still wasn't around much, though. She, like my father, was a workaholic on a quest for the American dream of financial freedom, and her commute to work, coupled with long working hours, kept her from home much of the time.

I don't remember much from this period, but I do remember the first time I got badly hurt. It wasn't long after we moved to Katy. My sister and I were fighting, the way kids do, and she backhanded me. I tumbled backward off the couch and struck my head against a huge, ugly clay pot, resulting in both the pot and my head being split open. I couldn't feel any pain, of course, so I just remember being excited by all the blood and the fact that I'd broken this big clay pot. I didn't really get what all the fuss was about. I was taken to the hospital, where I got about twenty stitches, which I thought was cool, too; it all seemed like a pretty good adventure to me.

This was the mid-seventies when oil was booming and pretty much everyone in Houston was making money. We weren't wealthy by any means, but we were definitely upper middle class. Dawn and I had pretty much everything we wanted, from a material standpoint. I still remember the Big Wheel I had; until I outgrew it, I spent more time riding on that bike than I did walking on my own two feet.

My parents were doing well enough financially that they decided to move us out to the suburbs off Highway 6. We moved into a big house in a nice neighborhood and Mom and Dad worked even harder to cover the monthly bills. They hired a maid who came on Wednesdays to clean the house, and while there, she acted as our nanny. During the rest of the week, we took care of ourselves, cooking our own dinners and often tucking ourselves in at night.

The maid's name was Diretha, but we always called her Dorothea because it was easier. She was a really kindhearted African-American woman from East Texas—deep East Texas—and when she spoke, she ran her words together with such a deep accent, we could barely understand a word she said. She would talk, and we'd just smile and nod. She was a short, heavyset, apple-cheeked woman, and she wore her hair up in a long-outdated kerchief. A few things she said that we could understand were "Oh baby," "Oh honey," and "Oh Lordy" whenever we got up to something. We acted up plenty, but Diretha never disciplined us; I think she felt like it wasn't her place to do so. The funny thing is, she was so sweet we might actually have listened to her, provided we could understand what she was saying. She was always smiling or laughing, and she was generous with hugs, which made her the perfect person to be around two lonely latchkey kids. Dawn and I loved Diretha, and she seemed to love us.

Our parents worked until eight or nine o'clock most nights, left early in the morning, and weren't home a lot on weekends. Dad was around even less, because he traveled so much for work, and when he was home, he spent a lot of time locked in his office doing business. He almost always came home from business trips with some little present for Dawn and me. There is no doubt in my mind that this was my dad's way of showing affection. That's probably also why Christmases were such a massive event in our household. I can remember coming downstairs on Christmas morning to piles and piles of gifts—so many that my parents couldn't fit them all under the tree—stacked in every direction. My dad couldn't communicate his feelings or express affection in any physical way, but he could certainly buy gifts. I think I developed a kind of subconscious association between love and material things because that's how my dad operated.

There were some good times in my childhood, though. I remember when I was eight and we went back to Colorado on a ski trip. My mom and dad visited old friends and reconnected with their ski bum roots, and my sister and I played in the snow and learned to ski. It was my first visit to the mountains, and I fell in love with Colorado, snow, and skiing; it's a love that continues to this day. We all had a wonderful time, and the memory of that family trip has always stayed with me.

My sister and I basically raised ourselves, which means we ran around like little wild heathens and did whatever we felt like doing, whenever we felt like doing it. There were a bunch of other neighborhood kids who were in a similar situation, so we spent a lot of time running around together, roaming the neighborhood and making a lot of noise. It wasn't long before I earned a reputation as a "troublemaker," but I think my trouble-making was just a matter of wanting attention and quality time and parental involvement. It didn't work.

My dad's idea of parenting—and my mother's, too, to an extent—was putting a roof over our heads. If we had clothes and food and a few toys, their job was done. My dad wasn't the playing-catch-in-the-backyard kind of father, and I can't remember many hugs or any praise. That's the brand of parenting my parents had experienced as children and it probably never occurred to them to question it. So very early on, I began to have a sensation of being unimportant. I was very, very insecure, but instead of hiding, I did things to get attention. I wanted so badly to be noticed by my parents. Even as a young kid, I felt like something was missing inside of me. I felt like if I were better or smarter or more fun, they would want to spend time with me.

Their lack of interest didn't deter me from wanting them. When I was five or six years old, I sleepwalked down to the corner of our street in the middle of the night and sat waiting for my parents to come home. I often watched for them there in the evenings, because it was along their route home. A police officer came by at three or four in the morning and asked me what I was doing there. I kind of came to and realized what was happening, and I just told him the truth: I was waiting for my parents to come home. He stared at me for a moment with a blank expression on his broad, ruddy face. I don't know if his lack of reaction was because he didn't want to scare me or because it simply wasn't the strangest thing he'd heard that night. He drove me home in his patrol car, and I remember wondering if I had broken some law and would be taken to jail. When we stopped in front of my house, though, he just took me by the hand and walked me up to our front door. My dad was out of town on business, but my mom was home, so she woke up to the sound of insistent knocking and a policeman at the door. For some reason, neither the police officer nor my mother acted like it was a big deal that I was out on the street at three o'clock in the morning. She did seem relieved to see me. But I've always thought it said a lot about my emotional state as a child; in the back of my mind, I was always wondering, *Where are my parents?* I was looking for something to make me feel safe and secure.

The first time I got drunk, I was eight years old. To be fair, it was an accident. But then again, maybe I thought drinking like the adults would be a way for me to connect with the two adults who were the most important people in my life. My parents both drank pretty regularly, though I don't know if they were actually alcoholics. There was always liquor in our home and parties and things of that nature, but I was too young at the time to know the difference between drinking socially and drinking alcoholically.

So when I was eight, Mom and Dad took us to their favorite restaurant, Ninfa's, which we frequented. Ninfa's was a really popular Mexican restaurant in Houston, which has since spread all over the South. Part of what made the place popular, of course, was its extremely large, extremely strong margaritas. So, on this particular night at dinner, I kept sipping on my parents' brightly colored margaritas, which everyone thought was pretty funny right up until I passed out face-first in my plate of beans. Actually, I think they still thought it was pretty funny.

My second bout with drunkenness was a few months later. My parents were having a New Year's Eve party, and I began sneaking glasses of champagne that were meant for the guests. It was fun and challenging to dip my glass into the cold, bubbling champagne fountain without being seen. After a while, I realized no one was really watching me and I didn't have to sneak them, so I just played grown-up and drank my champagne until I passed out. It wasn't just curiosity this time, though; it was peer pressure, too. My sister and several of the other neighborhood kids drank, too. Dawn told me later that I had started acting pretty silly. I was talking nonsense and running around, bumping into things. She and the other kids separated me from the adults so they wouldn't get busted. The last thing I can remember is making trips up to the fountain, filling my glass, and then sitting around with the other kids drinking. Even though I passed out, the evening was kind of exciting; it felt like we were doing something only grown-ups did.

The third time I drank was a doozy. I remember stealing Everclear from my dad's liquor cabinet when I was eight, and sharing it with a couple of kids from the neighborhood. This time, I didn't just pass out; I threw up, horribly and violently, and *then* passed out. Before that happened, though, I remember running around the neighborhood with a few other kids I'd shared the Everclear with, and having a blast. This is my first memory of intentionally using a substance to change the way I felt and to have fun. I still remember that experience distinctly. I remember the feel of the liquor in my throat, and I remember throwing up and telling myself I would never drink again—or at least that I needed to figure out how to drink enough to get drunk, but not enough to throw up.

Most of the neighborhood kids I tagged along with were older than me; some were my sister's friends, and some were just other largely unsupervised kids who had a lot of time to play. I was always the smallest—pretty skinny and kind of short for my age—and with my blond hair, blue eyes, and freckles, I looked a lot more innocent than I was. I was only five or six when I became involved in vandalism with a few of the neighborhood kids. We set fire to some trash on the tennis courts, toilet-papered a few houses, and spray painted meaningless symbols on the 7-Eleven. We also started stealing stuff. It was, for the most part, stupid, pointless stuff that we didn't need—things out of people's yards and the like. When I was six, I had stolen money out of my mother's purse, and I remember parceling it out to the neighborhood kids, thinking it would make them like me. But this wasn't like stealing a few dollars from my mother's purse; it wasn't about what we actually stole, but just about doing something exciting with the other kids. My behavior was an attempt to fit in with the other kids, as well as get attention.

The kid living across the street was named Mitch, and even though he was two years older than me, we became good friends and we remain friends to this day. When I was really young and we had just moved into the neighborhood, I used to go over to his house, and when his parents answered the door I would ask if "friend" was there. I guess I've always had a hard time remembering names. Anyway, "friend" and I tended to get into trouble a lot when we were together. Mostly we ran around doing typical little boy things. We got ahold of a couple of BB guns once, and got in really big trouble after I ended up taking a BB in the neck.

To this day, though, Mitch claims that even though I was younger, I was always the instigator, always the one coming up with the ideas that were likely to get us in the most trouble. Considering how badly I wanted attention, from almost anybody, I think he's probably right, and because of my overwhelming loneliness, I was notorious for driving his parents crazy. Since Mitch was older than me, he would be at school during the day while I was still at home. I remember being bored a lot during this time, since Dawn was at school and, of course, my parents were working. I used to go to Mitch's house several times a day and ring the doorbell. Mitch's poor dad had a home office and had to listen to me ring the doorbell over and over. Eventually, he would give up and come downstairs to inform me that "friend" was at school.

My troublemaking wasn't confined to the neighborhood, of course. I had my fair share of trouble at school. My first principal in Houston was only the first of several principals who got tired of my misbehavior shortly after I arrived at his school. He thought I was devious; I prefer the term "mischievous."

Dawn and I rode the bus to school, but whenever my dad was home, instead of traveling for work, I would leave the house late and walk down to the bus stop really slowly, missing the bus on purpose so that my dad would be forced to take me to school. On the way, we always stopped at Dunkin' Donuts, because he's a doughnut junkie. We used to get these little old-fashioned chocolate doughnuts, and to this day, I can't pass one by; it reminds me of those times. That little half hour with my dad was a really big deal for me. I was always doing little things, like missing the bus, to try and get his time and attention.

Around this time, when I was nine, things started to change in our house. I knew things were off somehow, but I couldn't figure it out. Then my parents announced that they were getting a divorce and it all made sense. This was in the early eighties, and the economy was imploding. I'm not sure how my parents' finances were affected, but I think it was just an added stress on an already unstable marriage. Looking back on it, I don't remember my parents being any more affectionate with each other than my dad was with my sister and me, so I don't know how long they had been having problems, but I know the announcement was abrupt. All of a sudden, my parents were getting divorced, and we were moving.

As a kid, my reaction was predictable: I assumed it was my fault. I felt like it was all about me, and I turned that guilt and worry and shame inward. I was so afraid of losing what little family life I had experienced up to that point: the times when we went out to family dinners to celebrate birthdays and the family vacations and waking up on Christmas morning to open presents together. I knew those times were over, and I was afraid of what life would be like without them.

My parents informed my sister and me that we would be living with our mother in Livingston, which is about two hours north of Houston. I was very upset that we were moving so far away from my father and from everything and everyone I knew. The terms of the divorce were that my sister and I would spend every other weekend with our father, plus two weeks in the summer. Despite the arrangements, I remember being afraid that I was never going to see him again.

We moved into a small red brick house that my mother had rented, just on the outskirts of town. Mom continued to work in Houston, six days a week. She had a two-hour drive to get to work, and then a two-hour drive home, so her workdays were twelve to fourteen hours long, and for a while it seemed like she was never at home. Her mother, Lyle, moved in with us to help look after Dawn and me. She was a short, heavy woman with thick, Coke-bottle lenses that made her eyes look unnaturally large, and once in a while I'd catch a trace of her Australian accent. In many ways, she became our mother. She fed us, clothed us, took us to school, and even tried to discipline us on occasion. Unfortunately, she was a very bitter, hard woman who'd had a series of abusive marriages and whose children blamed her for miserable upbringings.

Her first husband, my mother's father, died when Mom was young, from complications from an injury received in action during WWII. He had met my grandmother in her native Australia and brought her home to the United States. My grandmother's second husband, Walter, my mother's stepfather, died of prostate cancer before I was born. Walter was a very abusive alcoholic whom Grandma never spoke of much and whom Mom only referred to with hate and disdain. After his death, Grandma remarried for a third time—again to an alcoholic. Her third husband ran their restaurant into the ground and depleted their retirement savings.

Life's disappointments had taken their toll on Grandma and drained her of any compassion or empathy she might once have had. She did not drink, her ways were set, and she rarely spoke in a kind or loving tone, making her a difficult woman to live with. At the time she moved in with us, Dawn and I didn't know our grandmother well, though we had seen her from time to time.

She kept her personal history close to her chest and rarely spoke of her past.

She had a little piece of land that my mother and father had bought for her in Hempstead (about an hour north of Houston) before they divorced, and occasionally we'd go out there for a visit. She lived in a little house with about ten acres of land and a barn where she kept chickens and a few cows. She had a black dairy cow that Dawn and I named Lacy; it was the sweetest, gentlest cow in the world. We would crawl all over her and jump from the fence onto her back, while she would just stand there and placidly chew her cud. We loved playing with Lacy and chasing the chickens around, so we had some good times out at that farm, but mainly with each other; our grandmother was never very friendly. Since she had never interacted with us much, we only had the barest of relationships with her. But her moving in with us wouldn't change that. We never understood her; she was a mean, unhappy old woman who felt she needed to share her misery with everyone around her.

Our first response to Livingston was culture shock. Moving from Houston—even though we had lived in the suburbs—to a small town, my first thought was, *Where's the rest of it?* Shortly after we moved, though, I made a new best friend named John, a cheerful Hispanic kid who lived down the street. John was a couple years older and a Boy Scout, and he taught me a lot about things to do in the country. We took hikes, went fishing, threw rocks, and did all the other outdoorsy things country boys do. We hit it off right away and became inseparable.

Prior to the move, my mother began dating a guy named Jim. Jim was the town veterinarian, and he was also a Vietnam vet; he had done two tours in the Special Forces. Needless to say, he scared the living daylights out of me. They hadn't been dating long before he moved in with us and started running the family military style. Because he had a more traditional schedule, he was around a lot more than my mother was.

Jim was like John Wayne on steroids. He was about six feet two, and had a bushy brown mustache and tattoos up and down both forearms. He had a deep, gruff voice and always smelled like the Swisher Sweets he smoked. Jim was yet another person in my life who drank like a fish. I don't think I ever saw him without a beer in his hand—or at least close by.

It didn't take him long to decide that I wasn't tough enough for his liking. Of course I was only nine years old and had never been to war, so that probably had a lot to do with it. He decided the best way to toughen me up would be to turn family life into boot camp. My sister and I were given daily chores around the house. We were also given tasks to do at his vet clinic every day after school—mostly things we weren't really big enough for. Jim used to always make me carry big five-gallon buckets of water to feed the animals in the pens. The bucket of water weighed more than half of what I did. Jim would walk behind me, yelling at me the whole way while I tried to keep from crying and spilling any water. And he communicated with us like a drill sergeant: "Why can't you carry that, you big baby? You're weak and lazy! Pick up the pace, little girl!"

Jim's constant short temper and verbal abuse took a toll on me very quickly. I already struggled with feelings of worthlessness, and he reinforced them by making it clear that he thought I was pretty much worthless, too. He regularly made fun of me for not being tough enough. I knew that no matter what I did, I'd never be tough enough for Jim, so I just did my best to stay out of his way. Subsequently, I spent as much time at John's house as I could, even though it wasn't air-conditioned, which says a lot when you live in Texas. John's family could never understand why I wanted to be at their house when I had air-conditioning and a color TV at mine. I just loved being around John and his parents and sisters, who were sort of my idea of a "real family." They ate dinner together every night, and talked and laughed with each other. They were happy people and had a very positive energy about them that I missed in my own home. Even though John's parents didn't speak any English, they treated me like family and allowed me to spend a lot of time at their house.

Easily the most trying time for me during Jim's reign was when I was caught stealing and eating a single piece of butterscotch candy in the grocery store. My sister told my grandmother on me while we were still in the store, and my grandmother made me go tell the manager what I had done and apologize to him. I didn't much mind doing that, but I dreaded what would happen when Jim found out about it. I thought about asking my grandmother not to mention it, but I didn't trust her, so I kept my mouth shut. When we got home, she told Jim that I had eaten a piece of candy in the store without paying for it. Jim decided he was going to punish me, and he started by asking me to go get his belt. When I brought it back, trembling from head to toe, he asked me if I wanted to take my punishment then, or if I wanted to think about what I had done. I thought, *What is this, a trick question?* It seemed like a no-brainer. Since I was scared to death of him whipping me, I told him I would like to think about what I had done first. Little did I know what that meant.

"Thinking about it" to Jim meant that I was to stay in my room, twenty-four hours a day, seven days a week, for one month. No TV, no books, no phone, no toys—only me and a notepad in which I had to write "I will not steal again" one thousand times a day. This happened during the summer, so I could hear my friends who wanted to play being turned away at the door. I was afraid they'd forget about me or that John would have a new best friend by the time I was free. I used the shower and bathroom connected to my room, and ate my meals alone. I was ordered to keep my blinds closed at all times, so I didn't see the outside world for a month; I was too scared of breaking the rules to even peep out the slats.

I slept a lot during the day to pass the time, but this often meant I would lie awake at night. My sleeping became so erratic that it made me a little delirious at times—that and the fact that I didn't have anyone to talk to, because another part of my punishment was that I was not even allowed to speak to anyone in the house unless it was to answer a direct question. I remember sitting in my room and listening to everyone else watch TV, talk, and eat dinner; it was the loneliest feeling in the world. Throughout the thirty days, I had a mixture of emotions. Sometimes it was rage over the injustice; sometimes it was depression and sadness from feeling lonely and worthless. I distinctly remember thinking I had really been abandoned. Thirty days of solitary confinement for a nine year old is a little extreme, if I do say so myself. Even in prison they let you go outside for an hour a day.

I think my grandmother enjoyed my punishment even more than Jim. I knew that she had told Jim instead of my mom because she knew I would get in more serious trouble. She resented the fact that she had to live with us and look after us kids. And she was angry with my parents for selling her farm when they divorced. She wanted to punish us all, and this was one simple way of punishing me.

This was a pretty traumatic experience all around, but the thing I remember most is feeling like I'd been betrayed by my mother. I could've expected something like this from Jim—he was a sociopath—but I almost couldn't believe she didn't step in, didn't say one word. I couldn't believe she had just handed all the power in our family over to this stranger.

One good thing came of this experience, though: it ended the childhood era of my sister and me telling on each other. Dawn had been the unwitting catalyst of this event by telling my grandmother that I had not paid for the candy I had eaten. After seeing what happened to me, she felt so guilty that she never tattled on me again. It also helped bring us closer, because we started to really stick together. In a lot of ways, it was us against them.

About six months into my mom's relationship with Jim, she met another man named Thomas. Thomas was in his last year at A&M, and he'd been doing an internship at Jim's veterinary clinic. My mom broke up with Jim—who moved out, much to the delight of my sister and me—and began dating Thomas. He was tall like Jim and sported a mustache, but he was pale, thin, balding, and a lot meeker than Jim.

Soon after that, my mother bought a house and twenty acres right on the Trinity River outside of Livingston, smack dab in the middle of a rancher's five-thousand-acre ranch. We went from rural to middle-of-nowhere rural. It was a thirty-minute drive to school, and our closest neighbor was at least two miles away. I was not happy about the change, as it was now next to impossible to escape to John's house. Our new place was beautiful—it was surrounded by trees and had a large pond right in the front yard—but I was too unhappy about being in the middle of nowhere to appreciate the beauty of it. I did get a wonderful dog, though: a Great Dane named Star. We went everywhere together, exploring the woods and the river. I even occasionally slept with her out in the doghouse.

I was continuing to have behavioral problems at school. In Houston, there had been no corporal punishment. Well, in Livingston, there was. I fancied myself the class clown, which all of my teachers quickly grew tired of, and I started to get paddled in the book room on a daily basis. I was around ten or so and had by this time regained the ability to feel pain. Well, after getting paddled every day for about a month, the message sank in—I don't know why it took a month, but it did. I straightened out and became a better student. I stopped being a discipline problem, I got along well with the other kids, and I started bringing home straight As.

Throughout all this time, my dad was not keeping up his end of the custody agreement. He was enjoying his newfound bachelorhood, or maybe it was a midlife crisis; whatever it was, it did not involve active parenting. He was doing a lot of dating and partying, and we weren't seeing him much at all. Occasionally, we would go down to Houston for a weekend visit. Visiting him mostly consisted of my sister and me goofing off at the neighborhood pool or playing with our friends, while our dad worked in his office. He kept the house as organized and as spotless as a museum, and it drove him crazy if we made any messes. He liked for us to be out of the house from the time we woke up until it was time for bed. This was nothing new to us, so we just found ways to keep ourselves entertained.

On the other hand, though, my mom was around a little bit more, because she and Thomas had decided to start up their own veterinary clinic, and she had quit her job in Houston. Starting a new business is pretty time-consuming in and of itself, but she no longer had a two-hour daily commute, so she was home a little more. And it wasn't all doom and gloom, of course. I can remember my mom taking my soccer team out for ice cream after a game or taking us to dinner to celebrate a good report card. But the truth is, those kinds of things were isolated events in a pretty lonely childhood. My grandmother was still living with us, and it was supposed to be her job to look after us, but as I've said, she was not a nice lady. Her only income was her social security, and she simply couldn't afford to live alone, so she was forced into the situation. She didn't want anything to do with us, and we didn't want anything to do with her, so we forged an unspoken mutual agreement to stay out of each other's way.

Thomas had started to become more of a daily presence in our lives. He was a fairly young guy, and while he wasn't particularly warm, he also wasn't militant and aggressive, as Jim had been, so my sister and I thought he was "nice enough." Pretty soon, he moved into our house, and he and my mother announced that they were getting married. I wasn't upset by this news. Their little wedding, Mom's third, was held in our backyard, and I was the ring bearer. We were on track to being one big, happy family.

Soon, we started going to visit Thomas's parents every so often. They lived in Cleveland, Texas, about thirty minutes from our house in Livingston, and his father, Weldon, took an interest in me and assumed the role of a grandfather-type figure. We'd go to their house on weekends, and Weldon would take me out hunting and fishing. He bought me my first rifle, a .22, when I was eleven, and let me shoot cans off his back fence. While this was standard stuff to a country boy, it was a big deal for an eleven-year-old city kid like me, who had never shot a rifle before.

Weldon was an alcoholic and drank pretty much nonstop, so part of what we would do was cruise around to bars together. Or rather I would go with him to all these little country watering holes and sit beside him while he drank. I'd sit on a barstool and eat beer nuts while he and his friends talked to each other or to me. They got a kick out of having a little kid in the bar, and I got a kick out of the attention. And it formed a little bit more of my skewed reality; I assumed that everybody was in bars all the time, everybody drank, and it was just natural.

My sister and I were continuing to grow closer, and she even let me hang out with her and her friends sometimes—a pretty big deal, considering I was ten and they were fifteen. One afternoon, she and her friend Karen went up to Thomas and my mother's room, and when I tried to follow, I was told I couldn't come. Naturally, I whined and complained and cajoled until they yielded and grudgingly allowed me to follow. That's the day I was introduced to pot.

We went upstairs and snuck some pot from the little stash of weed in the closet my mother and Thomas shared. I was shocked and disappointed to find out that my parents were doing drugs. In school and on TV, drugs were bad and dangerous. I lost a lot of confidence in my mom and Thomas when I saw that pot in their room, but then we went into the attic that was attached to their room, and my shock was overshadowed by the excitement of being a part of something mischievous with my sister and her friend. I wasn't as afraid of drugs as I was of being left out; I would do almost anything to avoid that. Though I didn't fully comprehend the significance of the moment, I knew it was a big deal—something beyond the pale of my usual mischief—and I remember being petrified, of what I didn't exactly know. When we got up to the attic, they didn't offer me any pot, and I didn't ask for any. I remember sitting on the hard floor, with my back against one wall, chatting with the girls and watching them grow increasingly giggly. I remember smelling that oddly sweet, rich, smoky scent for the first time and thinking it was strange and exotic, like nothing I'd ever experienced before. Fears notwithstanding, I was instantly attracted.

After that day, I was deemed cool enough to hang out with Dawn and Karen while they got high. After a month or two of watching them, I finally decided I wanted to try it myself. They didn't really want to let me and tried to tell me no, but I threatened to tell on them (which I would never have actually done, having learned that inadvertent lesson on sibling relations from Jim). Anyway, I eventually wore them down and they gave in. We drove our old pickup down a dirt road behind our house to get stoned. Dawn pulled over to the side of the road, and we rolled the windows down—it was too hot to leave them up, even if that would have increased our buzz. Dawn and Karen, on either side of me, lay on the seat and dangled their feet out the windows, and we passed one joint back and forth. Since I was in the middle, I ended up double-dipping on my share of the joint.

After a few minutes, I began to laugh uncontrollably. At first, the girls thought it was pretty funny, but I really couldn't stop laughing—I could barely breathe—and after a while, they got a little freaked out. Eventually, the laughter died down, much to our mutual relief, and we headed home, where I proceeded to eat everything within arm's reach. Luckily, like everything else I did, this escaped my parents' notice.

All things considered, I enjoyed my first experience with getting high; I liked that it didn't make me nauseated or tired, like drinking did. Thereafter, I continued to get high with my sister and her friends, usually once or twice a week. I had continued to drink off and on since my Everclear experience when I was eight, but more often than not, it ended up with me puking. I desperately craved the sensation of being high or drunk, and with pot I could escape without throwing up. More importantly, it took away that feeling I always carried with me—the constant worry about what people thought, the fear that I didn't fit in, the inability to feel comfortable in my own skin.

Before long, I began to spend a lot of time thinking about when I could get high next. My addiction really began to blossom and to consume me psychologically. By the time I was eleven, I was getting high daily, or at least as often as I could, and instead of playing outside, I spent a lot of time reading books and sitting around the house. Between the lethargy and the munchies, I started to get pretty chubby, though I did have a dirt bike and a go-cart that I'd ride around on sometimes. I had also started to get really into skateboarding, but there was no good surface for it at the house in the country, so I mostly did that in Houston. We would visit my dad on occasional weekends, and I would hang out with my old buddy Mitch. On one visit, I introduced Mitch to pot.

He and I, along with Dawn and Karen, all hung out in his backyard, getting stoned and drinking Boone's Farm wine while his parents were out at dinner. We sat in their hot tub and got drunk before getting stoned. The combination of wine, pot, and the hot tub made me puke, of course, but Mitch handled himself pretty well. They all stayed up partying while I slept it off in Mitch's room. The next day Mitch told me he thought pot was okay, and we got stoned again later that afternoon.

This was the early eighties, and new-wave fashion and music were really popular. I tended to sport the Houston style—long hair, checkered Vans, and parachute pants—which hadn't caught on in Livingston yet. There, everyone was wearing Wrangler jeans and cowboy boots. So as I entered junior high, and the kids began to splinter into cliques, I felt like the other kids thought I was weird, though John continued to be my buddy (I introduced him to pot, too) and my sister's friends liked me. In fact, I got along well with most girls, who found my uniqueness kind of cool and intriguing. But I ran into problems with guys and began getting into a lot of fights. I was having an identity crisis and really struggling to fit in. Being teased for my weight and the way I looked helped push me deeper into my insecurity, and I rarely felt comfortable with myself or my surroundings.

In addition to the issues I faced with my peers, things on the home front were getting dicey again. Thomas and I had been getting along okay, but we had not bonded in any fashion. He was just my mom's husband and we communicated very little. However, when I began to sport the new-wave look, he began to take an interest in me and not in a positive way. He took great delight in making fun of my hair and my clothes. On the surface, it was pretty harmless, but it did hurt not to be accepted by my new stepfather, especially since I had such low self-esteem to begin with. I already felt inferior to everyone else. His ridicule only heightened my feelings of isolation.

Though my mom didn't stand up to Thomas for me, she did stand up to the principal on my behalf. The school had complained about the fact that I came in one day with half my head shaved. She marched down there and asked the principal where in the rulebook it stated that I couldn't shave half my head. That was a really big day for me; I felt surprised and elated that my mom had stood up for me. What I didn't understand was why she could never do that with Thomas, and why she had never done it with Jim or my dad before that.

In seventh grade, I experienced yet another setback in the development of my self-image. I took an interest in football and played on the school team. I was already doing drugs, but they weren't yet affecting me physically. I was playing right guard and middle linebacker, and I was pretty good—good enough that they wanted to promote me to the eighth grade team a year early. To be on the eighth grade B team in seventh grade seemed like the biggest honor I would ever receive; it was a really big deal for me and had the potential to be a major esteem builder. The day the coach told me about it, I went home so excited I was practically vibrating; I couldn't wait to tell my mom and dad.

Being on the eighth grade team would require daily practices after school, Friday night games, and traveling. When I told my mom about it, she said that I couldn't do it because it would be too hard to drive me around all the time. The school bus didn't run out to where we lived, so my grandmother did all the shuttling of us kids. If I joined the team, I'd be getting out of school an hour and a half later than my sister and my grandmother couldn't return to get me. Well, she could, but they figured the extra thirty-minute drive would be too big an inconvenience, and since things at the vet clinics weren't good financially, the gas would be too expensive. I was so angry about this that I said to hell with football altogether. If I couldn't play on the eighth grade team, I didn't want to play at all, so I quit. I was just acting out, pouting, hoping my mom would recant. In the end, I only hurt myself, though.

When I was twelve, things around the house really started to change. Thomas hurt his back while loading a horse into a chute, and got the bright idea that he could prescribe himself veterinary drugs, so he began taking various animal tranquilizers for the pain. He became more and more withdrawn and much more verbally abusive to both me and Dawn. One day, the verbal abuse wasn't satisfying enough, and he progressed to the physical kind.

Thomas came home early one afternoon and found that I hadn't yet finished my chores. For whatever reason, he flew into a fit of rage, and before I could even react, he was punching me in the chest, stomach, and back with enough force to knock the wind out of me. Not only was I obviously in some real pain, but I was also terrified of being beaten up by a grown man. At some point, I was knocked to the ground where I just curled up, waiting for it to stop. After he finished making his point, or maybe just got too tired to continue, he went to bed. As soon as I caught my breath, I rode my bike to an old tumbledown shack about a mile from our house. The shack was just off our dirt road, so I knew my mother would drive by on her way home.

I sat on the floor of this oppressively hot, dusty shack, crying, until she came home several hours later. When I heard her car, I ran out and stopped her, and frantically explained what had happened. She didn't believe me. She told me to take off my shirt and show her where he'd hit me. Of course, any knowledgeable abuser knows that the chest and stomach are the best places to hit someone because it typically doesn't leave a mark. I don't know if Thomas was smart enough to have given it that much thought, but my torso was bruise-free, so my mom thought I was lying (or told herself I was). She told me to go home and go straight to my room. I don't think I was even mad at her; I just remember feeling dumbstruck and disappointed that the same woman who had marched angrily up to the school to defend my right to have a stupid haircut had decided that protecting her child from an abusive stepfather was less important than protecting him from a school principal. My sister believed me and we vented our frustrations by getting high that night.

At this time, I was still getting high daily. It was a way to escape, to dull my feelings of inadequacy and awkwardness, and, as far as I could tell, there was no downside; it didn't make me feel sick or hungover, like drinking did, and all the people I knew were doing it, so what could be the harm? I supported my habit by stealing money from my parents—or simply stole pot from my mom's secret stash. Obviously, my thirty days in solitary confinement for stealing hadn't made as much of an impression as Jim had hoped. I was still doing pretty well in school—mostly As and Bs—and the constant reading probably made up for whatever focus or concentration was lost to the pot.

One weekend, Thomas's cousin Jeff came to stay with us. He was in his early twenties, and had recently gotten out of the military. He didn't have a job and needed a place to stay, so he crashed at our house for a while. Because he was fairly close to our age and unemployed, he hung out with Dawn and me a lot. He taught me some martial arts and told stories about being in the military and traveling to different places. Being a twelve year old, I thought he was really cool and looked up to him. I think in addition to his inherent coolness, I was drawn to him because he was an adult who actually wanted to spend time with me, who sought me out and taught me things. I thought he might be someone who could be like a father to me, only cooler than my dad, and closer to my age.

While he was staying with us, he slept in my room. We shared the bed in my room, and one evening when I was feeling pretty lonely and insecure, I scooted closer to him and rested my back against his side. He threw an arm over me and gave me a hug, which was a reassuring gesture. As I began to settle in and drift off to sleep, I felt his hand slide down to my genitals. I freaked out and didn't know what to do, so I just kind of clammed up and curled into a ball, paralyzed by what was happening. When I scooted over, I was afraid he wouldn't stop. Thankfully, he got the message and left me alone. He fell asleep soon after, but I lay awake all night, terrified he'd do something else to me. I remember thinking, *Why did he do that to me? Is it my fault?* All I wanted was someone to protect me and make me feel safe, and what I got was someone trying to hurt me and take advantage of my neediness. From then on, while Jeff stayed with us, I slept in my sister's room. I don't remember what I told her, but I didn't tell her or anybody else what had actually happened for a long time. I don't think I spoke of it until I was fourteen or fifteen, when I was forced to have a couple of sessions with a therapist, due to trouble I had gotten in at school. Jeff stayed with us for probably another month, but he didn't speak of our encounter or seek me out again.

That was a pretty traumatic experience, and again I felt like I had done something wrong. It was a big thing in my head: shame and guilt and fear being all jumbled together and turned inward against myself. Besides, it's the egocentric nature of childhood to think everything's about you, right? I was too young to understand that I was the victim or to process what that meant. I remember feeling very alone with my secret, and I was deathly afraid of anyone finding out. My fear was that if anyone knew what had happened, they would blame me or say I was homosexual and make fun of me. Thankfully, Jeff moved on, and I never saw him again.

But things were getting worse and worse with Thomas. He and my mother were fighting a lot—always behind closed doors, but that didn't completely block out the yelling. He pretty much stopped going to work—he was always sleeping at the house during the day—and he acted very strange, talking to himself and overreacting to everything. One day, my mom told us very suddenly that she and Thomas were getting a divorce, and he moved out that same day. I don't think she gave us any details, and I don't think we asked for any; we were just glad to see him go.

I found out later that, among other things, he was addicted to ketamine, a horse tranquilizer that has hallucinogenic effects on humans. On the day Thomas and my mom announced their intention to divorce, he had taken my mother out on a boat on Lake Livingston. When they had gotten pretty far from the shore, he stopped the boat, took off all his clothes, and said,

"It's time for you to die." Luckily, my mother's a fighter. When he came after her with the intention of throwing her overboard, she pushed him away and wrapped her arms and legs around the metal post that supported one of the seats in the boat. He tried to pull her away from the post and screamed at her for about twenty minutes, but she held on tight. Finally, he exhausted himself and gave up. The ketamine was probably also starting to wear off, because without saying anything else, he put his clothes back on and drove the boat back to the dock. Needless to say, she didn't let go of that post until they were back at the dock, where other people were around. She successfully kept this information from us for many years. I don't know if it's a good thing or a bad thing, but Dawn and I didn't know what really happened between them until years later. All we knew at the time was that things were bad at home and new changes were coming fast.

Since Mom and Thomas had been business partners, things became very complicated financially. Their first veterinary hospital had expanded into three, but during the last few months before their divorce, Thomas hadn't been working much, and the business had started to go south. All three clinics had to be sold or shut down. My mom had used her credit and savings to get the clinics up and running in the beginning, so she was wiped out financially. She had to go back to working retail in Houston, fourteen hours a day, six days a week.

I was still smoking a lot of pot, but I was drinking more, too. At the parties I attended, the kids my age were more into drinking than smoking weed. My buddy John would get high with me sometimes, but he also preferred drinking. Although it wasn't my favorite form of intoxication, I still did it to feel high and fit in, even though it still made me sick nearly every time. What was important was the feeling of connection it gave me.

One evening after school, when I was probably thirteen, Dawn asked me if I had any pot. By that time, I was buying my own, from kids at school and some street dealers I'd learned about, so I didn't have to steal it from my mom as often. I had a joint, but I told her, "Look, if you want to smoke a joint, I'll smoke it with you, but I'm not just giving it to you." After pressuring me for a little bit, she finally told me that she was actually asking for our mom. Apparently, they had been getting stoned together. I was a little bit thrown, but again I said, "Well, if she wants it, then she's gonna have to smoke it with us, because I'm not gonna just give it to her." I think I was trying to be a tough guy, but mostly I wanted to make my mother come right out and admit what she was doing, even though I already knew. It was also a way of confessing to her that I was getting high, too—even though, again, I'm sure she knew.

So I got my little stash out of my sock drawer and went outside to smoke pot with my big sister and my mother. It was totally surreal and not in a good way. In fact, it was probably the most awkward situation I'd ever been in or will ever be in. We all stood outside on the porch, me in the middle, with my mom and Dawn on either side. I lit the joint, took the first drag, and passed it to my mother. We stood in complete silence, passing the joint back and forth, inhaling self-consciously, and not looking at each other. Now I knew she did drugs, and she knew I did drugs, and everything was out in the open. We all smoked together every so often after that, but purely out of expediency. It was never as much fun as it was when I was with my friends or my sister, but it served the purpose when one or another of us was out of pot.

Eventually, I figured out where my mom was getting the pot from, or I think I did anyway. There was a guy that we used to go see from time to time. His name was Ronnie, and he was a friend of my mom's. Ronnie was a stereotypical biker guy—he had a super long beard, long hair, and owned a motorcycle shop. He may have been my mom's dealer, but he was a very nice guy. I spent a lot of time hanging out at the motorcycle shop with Ronnie and my mom while they drank together. He had a big keg and a refrigerator, and they'd sit and drink beer and shoot the breeze. This guy was just nice to me—no demands, no repercussions, no expectations. He always made me feel like I was the center of attention, and I didn't get that from anyone else, so I loved it there. He used to ask me to take test rides on the dirt bikes he repaired. I know now that he didn't need me to test out the bikes; it was just another way for him to make me feel accepted. He also used to let me have stuff that I liked from his shop for free, but that's not what I liked about visiting him. I liked the fact that he made me feel important during a time in my life when I was needy, lonely, and lost.

All of these events occurred during the few weeks before school ended that year and I began my summer vacation in a massive state of confusion and wild abandon. In order to prepare for the summer, one of my friends and I stole some jewelry and a stereo from one of his neighbors and sold it to buy pot. We skipped school and crawled through an unlocked window while the owners were at work. Then we traded the stuff to a dope dealer in town. We were able to get an ounce of pot each, more than I'd ever had at one time, and I thought it was pretty cool. I rolled the whole ounce into one hundred joints and thought, "Now I am ready for summer."

CHAPTER 2

That summer, I stayed with my dad in Houston for the longest time ever—two full months. I'm pretty sure my mom had pressured my dad to keep me for a longer stay, either because she wanted him to be a better father or because she wanted a break. I was really hoping that this would be the summer when my dad and I would get close and become pals— surely he and I could hang out together enough to bond while I lived there for two months. I also decided that I had enough pot to smoke at least one joint a day and I was going to stay high all summer. How I thought I was going to spend all this time with my dad and stay stoned all the time is a mystery to me. Either I didn't think the equation through, or I knew deep down that there wasn't going to be a lot of father-son bonding time.

Visits with my dad usually consisted of him dropping Dawn and me off at the movies, the mall, or a friend's house, and picking us up at night. My sister and I used to spend all day at the movies, sneaking from one film to the next and trying not to get caught. In Livingston, there was only one little theater that showed one out-of-date movie at a time, so it was heaven to go to a big theater in Houston, where six or seven of the latest movies would be playing.

This particular summer, the summer I turned fourteen, my sister was eighteen and had just graduated from high school. She was staying with her boyfriend, and I was staying with my dad and his girlfriend. The economy had taken a downturn and my father had moved into a new house within biking distance of my old neighborhood and my friends. He was dating a friend of my Aunt Cathy's, and they had moved in together. His girlfriend's name was Gail, and she was about twenty years younger than him, but she was always nice to my sister and me, and we decided we liked her pretty well.

Aunt Cathy lived close by, and her two sons, Chad and Ryan, were staying with her for the summer. Growing up, I had spent time with Chad and Ryan on occasion, and we got along well. Chad was a year older than me and Ryan a year younger. During that summer visit, I hung out with my cousins, skateboarding and learning to play tennis. Teen night clubs were pretty popular then, so my cousins and I would go to the clubs on weekend nights to try and meet girls. This was the era when *Miami Vice* was the height of cool and we all wore goofy outfits in pastel colors, like pink and aquamarine. We thought we were hot stuff and tried our best to be cool. We also spent a lot of time at amusement parks, like AstroWorld and Fame City, on the weekends.

Chad and Ryan lived with their father in Michigan during the school year, and Aunt Cathy wanted them to enjoy their visit, so she was good about keeping us entertained. As far as I knew, my cousins were not into drugs and I didn't know if they would tell on me, so I mainly smoked pot by myself at night, when I could sneak out. My mom either hadn't told my dad that I used drugs or else he chose not to notice. Most likely, both of those scenarios are true. I'm sure my mom wouldn't want anyone to know we got high together, and my dad was the epitome of self-absorbed. He spent almost every waking moment thinking about his job, his house, his car, and his appearance. From my perspective, there wasn't much room for him to think about anyone other than himself.

When I got to Houston, I started looking for a part-time job, at my father's request, in order to have money to pay for my own stuff, and also to give me something to do to keep me out of his hair. I found a job after a couple weeks, working in the warehouse of a place that sold welding materials. When I heard about this job, I submitted an application and then proceeded to call three times a day to ask if they would hire me. After about a week of this, the boss said he would hire me just because I was so persistent (a nice way to say that I was driving him nuts). I worked from ten in the morning to two in the afternoon, Monday through Friday, packing boxes, labeling bottles, and sweeping the warehouse. They paid me four dollars an hour, which was a lot of money in my mind. I really wanted the money from the job so I could buy stuff and go have fun, and I enjoyed working and getting a paycheck every Friday because it made me feel independent and like an adult. The warehouse was about five miles from my house and I rode my bike there every day, which was about an hour and a half round trip. This was good because after I began smoking pot, I didn't get much exercise, and I had become somewhat overweight. The bike rides started to slim me down, which improved my self-image.

About a month into the summer, my old neighbor Mitch came home from a summer trip and we started hanging out again. Since he was a couple years older than me, he already had his driver's license. His parents let him drive his dad's custom van, which we thought was a pretty cool ride; it even had a refrigerator in the back. I looked up to Mitch because he was older, taller, and he'd been my fashion link to the big city up to that point. I was known to borrow his clothes and conveniently "forget" to return them. I guess Mitch tolerated this because we had been friends for so long and he had learned to accept my shenanigans.

Mitch picked me up one afternoon and we went to the mall to hang out and look at girls—one of our favorite pastimes. While we were there, we saw some kids Mitch knew from around the neighborhood; their names were Jay and Donnie. I vaguely remembered them from when I had lived in Houston, but they were eighteen or so, almost five years older than me. Somehow, the topic of pot came up and I proudly produced my big bag of joints. Everybody was fired up at the sight and we decided to go straight to Jay and Donnie's apartment to get stoned. The four of us showed up at the apartment and Jay pulled out a huge bong and said, "Let's unroll some of the joints and smoke out of the bong." I thought I was cool for having rolled so many joints, but Jay and Donnie were pretty advanced pot smokers and they insisted on using the bong.

I was immediately nervous. This was new to me, and these guys obviously knew what they were doing. I was excited to be around these older guys from the neighborhood, who had their own apartment, dressed in fashionable clothes, and carried themselves with an air of confidence. I immediately thought they were incredibly cool and wanted to make a good impression. After Jay and Donnie each took hits off the bong and showed us how to do it, Mitch took his first hit. He must've screwed up somehow, because he began coughing and blew snot everywhere, which we all found pretty hilarious. I tried it next and took it a little slower to make sure I didn't repeat Mitch's mistake. After just a couple hits, we were all stoned. I figured out pretty quickly why these guys liked the bong—it got us stoned a lot faster than a joint. A couple hours later, Mitch and I headed out, having agreed to hook up with Jay and Donnie again in a few days. I felt like I was now a part of a very cool group of guys.

While we were with Jay and Donnie, they told us about a cool new drug called ecstasy, which they touted as the best drug ever. Jay said it would make us feel happy and talkative and that we would have a blast on it. Mitch and I discussed it. Mitch said he'd heard it was pretty cool, so we decided to buy some. We planned to try it together with some girls that we were taking to AstroWorld that weekend. I was happy to have new, really cool friends, and I was glad Mitch was back so that I had a friend to party and get high with. Even at thirteen, I knew there was nothing cool about sitting around getting high alone.

So the big night arrived, and Mitch pulled up to my dad's house in the custom van, with the refrigerator full of wine coolers and beer. After he picked me up, we went to his girlfriend's house to pick up the rest of the crew. I remember thinking how unbelievably cool these people seemed to me. I tried to feel like I fit in, but I never really felt comfortable. When I was in the city, I felt like a backward country kid, and in the country, I felt like the weird city kid who stood out. This out-of-place feeling stuck with me everywhere I went. When I was stoned or drunk, it became a lot easier to feel like I fit in, but sometimes even the drugs and alcohol didn't work. That night would prove to be a whole different story.

When we arrived in the big parking lot at AstroWorld, we each took half a pill, which was the amount Jay suggested for our first time. It was supposed to kick in after half an hour and the effects usually lasted about six hours. As soon as we'd taken the ecstasy, we headed to the main gates and waited in line to get our tickets. We had heard that smoking clove cigarettes helped get the buzz going, so we were all smoking while we waited in line. This was my first time to smoke cigarettes as well, though I'd had plenty of experience smoking weed. About thirty minutes after we had taken the ecstasy, while waiting in line, it started to hit me. My vision became grainy, and when people around me were talking, it sounded like I was in a tunnel; their voices sounded echoey and far away. My heart began to race, and it felt like the whole world was vibrating around me. It was so intense at first that I felt nervous, but then the euphoria kicked in and my apprehension fell away. I felt very energetic, like I was moving faster than normal and could have covered every inch of that park at the speed of light. I remember getting a big grin on my face and suddenly feeling as if everything in the world was perfect. It seemed to hit us all at about the same time, and we just stood there, looking at each other and giggling. I was intensely happy. This was by far the best sensation I had ever felt, either high or sober.

This effect continued through the night. We spent the time riding the rides and talking and laughing with each other.

Everything was perfect and we all fell in love with each other—and the spell of ecstasy. We agreed it had been given a good nickname: "the love drug."

When we got home, the effects began to wear off, and after getting stoned in Mitch's backyard, I slept over at his house. That was my first introduction to pills, and it was an amazing experience. Afterward, Mitch and I decided we needed to hang out with Jay and Donnie more so that we could do ecstasy again.

The next week, I called Jay, and he came and picked me up so I could hang out with him. We ended up sitting around and getting stoned together. It was really nice having someone older show an interest in me. I was still searching for a role model, and Jay seemed like someone I could look up to. He invited me to go out with him and some other people that weekend to party and do some acid. I was nervous because I had heard of acid, and it seemed like a pretty hard drug. I knew of people who'd had bad experiences on acid. But I agreed to go, and Jay said he'd pick me up that Friday night.

When Friday came, he was running a couple of hours late. I was upset, thinking he wasn't going to come. My paranoia kicked in, and I thought he'd decided it was lame to hang out with a thirteen-year-old kid (although I'd told them I was fifteen). My dad made things worse by saying, "What made you think those people would want to hang out with you, anyway?" Of course, he didn't know Jay and his friends, but the comment only added to my self-consciousness, and I've never forgotten those words. They were the same ones I always asked myself.

Eventually, Jay arrived and we took off. I was so relieved he had shown up that I was on top of the world from the minute we left the house. He said we were going to meet some people at their apartment and then go out. Jay had brought his girlfriend, June, and his friend, KC, with him, and when we got to their friend's apartment, we all got stoned and took some acid. It was in paper form and I only took about a half a hit, just a little square of paper that they told me to put under my tongue. It was an uncomfortable experience to hang out with these eighteen-year-old kids at their apartment when I was just thirteen. I'd been around older kids all of my life, and everyone thought I was older and more mature than I really was, but I still felt like a fish out of water. Fortunately, Jay always treated me like I was one of his close friends, and that helped me feel more relaxed when I was with him.

Thirty minutes after I took the acid, I started feeling antsy and restless, and I asked Jay when we were leaving. The acid was taking effect, but it wasn't euphoric, like the ecstasy had been. Soon, we went to a restaurant to eat, drink, and hang out—though mostly we just drank. Jay and his friends kept asking if the acid was hitting me, but I kept thinking it wasn't—until I started talking to the waiter, who I thought was behind me. Jay laughingly informed me that I was talking to the air. Everyone laughed about it, and I joined in. That was my first hallucination.

After that, I acknowledged that the acid had definitely hit me. We hung out at the restaurant for a few more hours and drank some more and talked. We were all too young to drink legally, but one of the people in our group worked at the restaurant, so we were able to drink all night. When I got home, I went to bed, and in the quiet of my room, the effects of the acid felt stronger; everything seemed way too bright, and I saw tracers and spots of color behind my eyes every time I moved. I lay in bed for hours, trying to go to sleep, but I'm pretty sure I just tossed and turned all night.

While we were drinking at the restaurant, Jay had invited me to go to a club the next night and hang out; of course I didn't turn that offer down. In order to go, I lied and told my dad I was going to stay at Mitch's house; that way, I could stay out all night and sleep at Jay's apartment. Mitch was going to summer school (his mother, a teacher, made him take summer classes to get ahead) and his mother was the overprotective type, so he wasn't able to goof off with us all the time. I would have liked to have had him around more, but he still made for a good alibi, so I frequently told my dad I was staying over at his house.

Once again, Jay was late picking me up and that same panic hit me all over again. I remember thinking maybe I had acted stupid or said something dumb the night before and he didn't want to have anything to do with me. I would later find out that he was busy picking up and delivering ecstasy and acid all night. I was relieved when he finally arrived to get me and we went to the new apartment he and June were living in. We all took some ecstasy and then Jay, June, KC, Chris (a new person I had never met), and I all got ready to head out. They were all dressed up and I thought it was possible that they were the coolest people on the planet. I didn't really have any cool club clothes, so Jay took me in his closet and hooked me up with an outfit. Now I felt ready to roll with these guys in style.

In the car on the way to the club, the ecstasy started to hit me and it was just as good as the first time. I felt like I was on top of the world. I talked everyone's ears off while we drove down the street with the music loud and the top down on June's convertible. I loved everyone and this was promising to be the most amazing night ever. When we arrived at the club, it was packed—the line to get in wrapped all the way around the side of the building. I worried that we would be stuck in line all night and I wondered how I was going to get into an "eighteen and up" club with no ID. Jay told me not to worry because he had everything handled. He was always very cool like that.

When we got out of the car, we all walked to the front of the line where Jay seemed to know the doorman. They spoke for a moment, and to my amazement, he let us in without paying or even looking at our IDs. When we got inside, I felt like I was living out a scene from a movie. Everyone was dancing, the music was loud, the lights were dim, and it seemed like the crowd parted for us as we walked through the club. It was like being a rock star. That sensation was partly the ecstasy, but I soon found out that Jay and his friends were well-known there.

We walked to a seating area in the back of the club, and the people sitting there got up and left so we could all sit down. Immediately, KC and Chris went to work. They circulated the club, taking patrons' money and giving them Flintstones Vitamins and safety pins in return. They then sent their customers over to two new people who'd just arrived, who exchanged the pins and Flintstones for ecstasy and acid. Jay explained the process for selling the drugs and I was blown away by the whole thing. I just sat on the couch and watched everything going on around me in amazement. Once again, I felt like I was living in my dream world. It was awesome hanging out with these people who acted like they owned the place and got treated like royalty. They didn't wait in lines, people moved out of their way when they saw them coming, and everyone seemed to know who they were.

The night flew by, and the next thing I knew, it was four in the morning and the club was closing. We went to Chris's apartment with a bunch of amazing-looking girls and some more of Jay's friends. We all got stoned, and I watched them count the thousands of dollars they earned from selling drugs at the club. It was more money than I had ever seen before. I knew right then and there that I wanted to be just like Jay. I wanted to dress cool, have long hair, hang out at clubs, and sell drugs. Of course, the pretty girls and money would be a part of that package. I thought that if I was like Jay, then people would like and respect me. I had such low self-esteem that I was instantly attracted to what was happening around me. I decided I would ask Jay to set me up in the business.

We headed home around dawn. The ride back to Jay's apartment was surreal. I had just experienced what I thought was the most incredible night of my life, and I couldn't wait to do it all over again. We all fell asleep at Jay's around eight in the morning, and I slept all day. When I woke up, it was dark outside. It was such a bizarre feeling to sleep through an entire day and I was a little panicked because it was Sunday night and I needed to get home. I arrived home at ten and my dad was mildly annoyed that he had not heard from me. I came up with some story about where I had been all day. Of course, he bought it, because he wasn't really concerned and probably just wanted to get back to watching TV.

The next day was a Monday, and I had to go to work. Feeling awful, I headed in. I was tired and hungover, and I spent the whole day feeling bummed out because my summer visit was coming to an end. That weekend would be my last in Houston, and I was not looking forward to returning to Livingston. I worked my shift in a depression and went home to sleep it off.

I had spent a lot of time with my sister that summer, along with the guy she was living with, David. He became a big brother in a sense—a big brother who taught me how to do dangerous, illegal stuff. He taught me how to drive, despite the fact that I had recently turned only fourteen, and I drove on the freeways and all around the city. He taught me about various drugs and getting high, and the best way to roll a joint. Dawn began to get heavily into a variety of drugs that summer, including cocaine, ecstasy, and acid, and she did them with her boyfriend. Since I liked hanging out with my sister, the rest just followed. It was a very dysfunctional relationship. Toward the end of the summer, I brought some ecstasy over to her and David, and we all got high together.

My last Saturday in Houston, I went to the beach with Jay and Donnie. We took acid and surfed and hung out all day. It was a blast. I was really hooked on the life these guys were living and the life I lived when I was with them. That night, we went back to the club we'd gone to the weekend before, and pretty much repeated the last experience we'd had there. The drugs, power, girls, and money were completely captivating. That night, I set it up with Jay that I would sell acid and ecstasy when I got back home. He was going to front me the drugs, and I would pay him when I sold them all. This would be my first experience with selling, and I looked at it as an opportunity. Someday, I was going to be like Jay.

I was looking forward to my new role as local dealer, but I was still pretty bummed about returning to Livingston, especially since Dawn would not be returning with me; she was moving to Houston permanently. This was really hard for me because I felt like I was losing my sister. Not only was she my best friend, but she had always been the person who looked out for me and took care of me, so it was like losing my best friend, mother, and party buddy all at once. We did everything together and were very close, so I was definitely sad about her moving. However, when I got home, something happened that made me feel a lot better.

Prior to their divorce, my parents had been friends with a married couple who lived in our neighborhood. Their names were Bobbi and Gerry, and they were terrific people. They were very kind and made me feel good about myself, which was a rarity. Before my parents divorced, we all used to go over to their house on a regular basis. Dawn and I swam in their pool and played while the grown-ups talked and drank. Bobbi and Gerry were always very accommodating and tried to make sure my sister and I had fun. They had a knack for making people feel welcome and special. I guess that's one of the reasons my parents enjoyed spending time with them as well.

They had moved away from Houston before the divorce and we hadn't seen them for a while, but that summer, I found out from my mom that they had bought a waterfront home on Lake Livingston and were down for a visit, along with their two daughters, Heather and Shannon. Heather was about Dawn's age and she and Dawn had been best friends. Shannon was my age, but we had never been very close. I hadn't spoken to any of them in five years.

I found out that they'd been down the whole summer and there was not much time left to see them before they were to head back to California. My mother asked if I wanted to go visit them and spend the day at the lake. It seemed a lot better than moping around the house, so I went. All that bike riding had helped me get nice and trim, and I was looking pretty good; for the first time in as long as I could remember, I didn't get the chills at the thought of taking off my shirt to go swimming. I still felt insecure about myself, but not being fat anymore meant I had one less thing to worry about.

Somehow, I had expected Shannon to still be the nine year old she'd been when I had last seen her, but she sure wasn't; she had turned into a beautiful, curvy, fourteen-year-old girl. When I got to the lake house, she climbed out of the water, dripping wet in a tight bathing suit, and gave me a hug. I sure was glad I'd been riding that bike all summer. I developed an instant crush the moment I laid eyes on her.

She invited me to go swimming and off we went to the lake while our parents stayed home and got hammered. We floated a tube out on the water and took turns being on the inside, while the other person hung on to the outside. As we were floating and flirting, Shannon wrapped her legs around my midsection provocatively. I leaned forward and we began kissing. It was pure bliss. This was my first time to really kiss a girl. I had given girls the occasional peck on the lips before, but this was serious, all-out kissing. I thought, *I'm gonna lose my virginity to this girl.* After we finished swimming, we went inside and asked if I could spend the night. We hadn't discussed having sex, but I think we'd both planned it out. Our parents said I could stay, so Shannon and I spent the rest of the day hanging out and flirting.

When it was time for bed, they made a space for me on the floor in the room where Shannon and Heather both slept. Before bed, Shannon and I had made a plan for her to come down and lie with me after her sister fell asleep. So, I lay on that floor waiting for what felt like an eternity, the anticipation killing me. Finally, I went over to her side of the bed and saw that she had fallen asleep. Well, I had no intention of letting it go at that, so I woke her up to see if she was still interested. To my great relief, she was. She got up, very quietly, and we lay down together on the floor. We kissed for a few minutes, and then she began to take off her clothes. My heart was beating a mile a minute. I couldn't believe I was about to have sex for the first time.

She had an amazing body, and she looked so beautiful. I quickly took off my clothes and got on top of her, as if I knew what the heck I was supposed to be doing. I didn't even have a condom, but that was the last thing on my mind. I had seen movies in which people had sex, but I didn't know what to do or where exactly everything was supposed to go. Apparently, this was not Shannon's first time, because she took charge, and I just followed her lead. It was the most amazing, exciting sensation—even better than ecstasy. We made love over and over, all night, until the sun started to rise and she climbed back into bed with her sister. I was instantly in love with Shannon, and I couldn't wait until morning so I could see her and talk to her.

We slept late, of course, and then woke up Sunday morning and went swimming again. That evening, we asked if Shannon could come over to my house to "play." Our parents, utterly clueless, agreed. Shannon's family was returning to California on Monday, so this was to be our last night together. It was an exact repeat of the night before. It was wonderful. When it was time for her to go home, we made a plan to call each other every day, and we kissed good-bye. Despite my dissatisfaction with having to return to the country and school, those nights with Shannon were the perfect ending to a summer of fun, pleasure-seeking, and blissful irresponsibility.

I started high school soon after. I didn't really know what to expect, but I was looking forward to my new dealer status and I now had a girlfriend I thought I loved, so I wasn't dreading it. I started making friends with the kids who did drugs, most of whom were older and had their own cars. Being a dealer made me very popular, at least with this group. I felt powerful and protected, like no one could touch me. I became best friends with a kid named Joe and we'd hang out together and get high every day after school. I was still friends with John, but he wasn't as into drugs as I was, so we didn't hang out as much. I continued to call Shannon in California, but eventually she stopped calling me back. I was pretty depressed about this rejection, but I was enjoying my new life too much to be down for long. I decided to just concentrate on what was going on in Livingston.

My mother had started dating a guy named Harry, who lived in Shepherd, a very small community about ten minutes south of where we lived. Harry had a large house on a five-thousand-acre ranch and owned some oil wells that had made him a lot of money. Harry was a tall guy with silver hair who liked to drink, hunt, and play poker. He was fairly loud and overbearing, but he wasn't ever mean to me. He mainly ignored me, which doesn't surprise me, since I was just the son of his girlfriend and I wasn't exactly brimming with affection toward him either. Harry had two sons from his previous marriage, and his older son, Richard, lived with him, while his younger son lived with his ex-wife in Dallas. Richard and I got along pretty well because I soon found out he did drugs, and so we occasionally got high together. After a while, my mom moved in with Harry, and with Dawn gone, it was just my grandmother and me in Livingston. She cooked, cleaned, and drove me to school in the mornings and that was the extent of our interaction. We still didn't get along.

Aside from my academics, I was free to do whatever I wanted, which usually entailed getting stoned with my friends after school. I actually remember having my grandmother drive me to get pot after school a few times a week. I would tell her I needed to go get books or homework assignments from a friend, when I was really picking up pot from a dope dealer in town. She was either clueless or too self-absorbed to notice what was going on.

Most of the kids in my high school didn't know what ecstasy and acid were, so I introduced them to these new drugs. One of my customers, a kid named Jimmy, claimed that the ecstasy I'd sold him was no good, and we got into a fight in gym class. After a little scuffling and a couple of swings, the fight got broken up and we agreed to meet after school to finish it. A friend of mine named PJ had decided he wanted to be my bodyguard—when you have drugs and other people want them, you suddenly have a lot of friends—and he planned on being the one to finish the fight after school. Well, after school let out, Joe, PJ, and I drove to the fire tower a few miles from school—along with most of the school, because word had gotten around. PJ beat the hell out of Jimmy and I actually felt really bad for the guy, but it did give me some clout at school. Nobody messed with me after that.

On the way back from the fight at the fire tower, PJ and I were riding with my buddy Joe, and as we rounded a corner, we saw a car stopped in the road ahead of us. We swerved into the left lane to avoid it. The instant we swerved,

I saw an oncoming car, and before we even had time to do more than register the fact, we had a head-on collision. I grabbed the dashboard and braced for impact. The collision was deafening and the next thing I remember was thinking I had knocked out my teeth because I felt all these sharp things in my mouth. Instinctively, I began to spit them out, and then I realized it was pieces of the dashboard. I guess I'd had my mouth open when my face slammed into the dash and I took a bite of the plastic. I started laughing hysterically when I realized what had happened. That is, until the shock wore off and I realized I had a dislocated shoulder and a bunch of cuts and bruises. Joe's face had hit the steering wheel and his teeth had cut a huge hole in his lip. PJ was in the back, and he had only been slammed into the front seat. None of us had seat belts on, and we probably should have been killed. Pretty soon, an ambulance carted me off to the hospital where they set my shoulder and sent me home with my mother. I remember the police and ambulance driver talking about how lucky we were to be alive.

Soon after that, I talked my mom into letting PJ move in with us because his mother had kicked him out of the house. PJ's mom was an alcoholic who lived alone and PJ got in the way of her boyfriends when they came over. He got into a fistfight with one of the boyfriends and that was when she kicked him out. I was relieved not to be alone with my grandmother anymore. PJ and I would sneak out a lot at night and steal the family car, just to drive around aimlessly and get high.

For months, life went on like that—getting high, making average grades, and selling drugs. Whenever I ran out of merchandise to sell, Jay would come up, bring me a new batch and we'd hang out. On the surface, life was okay, but I still felt empty and worthless. Drugs helped me cope with those feelings, or at least helped me ignore them. My use and reliance on drugs continued to escalate and add to my feelings of worthlessness. It was all too overwhelming—not feeling loved by my dad (whom I hadn't seen since the summer), feeling ashamed about the abuse I'd endured, having an absentee mother, and dealing with all of the other turmoil in my life. I developed a rage and hatred for myself and everything around me. I felt like life was miserable unless I could escape by getting high.

Midway through my freshman year, the bank foreclosed on our house, and my mother announced that we were all moving in with Harry (well, all of us but PJ; he was on his own). I wasn't thrilled about this because I barely knew the man, and I was frustrated about once again having to move to a new area where I had no friends. My already bad attitude got worse.

My grandmother was able to move into a house nearby, rather than live with us, so the move wasn't as bad as I had anticipated, but I was still really angry. My drug and alcohol use increased even more. In fact, I was going to school high and staying high or drunk most of the day. I was taking acid and ecstasy several times a week, along with getting stoned every day. Over time, the amount I needed to ingest to get high had increased exponentially. Whereas I used to take half a hit of ecstasy or acid in the beginning, I now had to take two or three hits to get the same effect. I was beginning to use more than I was selling, and I would steal money from Harry's wallet just to keep up with my use.

Soon after we moved, though, I made friends with a classmate named Kevin. Kevin had a blue Chevy Nova, and he drove us everywhere. One weekend when we were drunk and driving around on some dirt roads, he spun out of control and flipped his car two and a half times, landing upside down. Neither of us had a seat belt on and yet we both miraculously walked away with only minor cuts and bruises. We quickly threw all the beer cans away and hid the pot before the cops and his grandparents came to the scene. I was getting into car accidents on a regular basis, and I didn't even have my license yet. I was lucky I was never seriously injured.

That summer, my dad moved to Dallas. I was desperately unhappy about this, because Dallas was four hours away and I barely saw him when he was two hours away. Plus, I would no longer be able to go down and hang out with my Houston friends. Right before he moved, though, he allowed my friend Kevin and me to come down and stay with him for a few days in Houston. That was when I was introduced to cocaine for the first time. While Kevin and I were hanging out in my dad's home office one afternoon, I went snooping through my dad's briefcase and saw a little plastic baggie full of white powder.

Dawn had told me once that our dad did cocaine, so even though I'd never seen coke before, I immediately knew what it was. I showed it to Kevin, and we decided to take some down to the neighborhood pool where we could go into the bathroom and snort it. We brought a straw from home so that we'd have something to snort it with. I'd seen people snort coke on TV and knew the basics of how it was done.

This would be my first experiment with what I consider to be one of the most evil substances on the planet. It burned my nasal passages and then almost instantly made my face feel numb. I started feeling really amped up. My heart raced, and I felt shaky. The sensation was not that great compared to ecstasy, because I didn't feel a sense of well-being. For some reason, we continued to snort more and more until all that we'd brought was gone. Even though it wasn't that fun or pleasant, we went straight back to the house to get more from my dad's stash; it was like we were both instantly addicted. What we experienced was a craving. It was like the need to drink water after having sweat profusely from exercise or being in the heat. Coke was all we could think about, and without it we felt cranky and restless. My dad had taken the baggie out of his briefcase while we were gone, and we looked everywhere, but couldn't find it. We were totally bummed, and coming down off the high was a miserable experience. Although we tried, we never did find any more, so we spent the rest of the weekend getting stoned and hanging out at the mall. I didn't get to hang out with Mitch, Jay, or Donnie that weekend, and I was really disappointed.

After that weekend, we went back to Shepherd, and I continued to create chaos any way I could as a way of expressing my frustration and anger. I would talk back to everyone, neglect to do my chores, stay gone from the house for extended periods of time without anyone knowing where I was, and basically do anything else I could to act out. I went to school, and I continued to sell drugs and get drunk and high all the time. At home, I kept away from my mother and Harry as much as possible. They didn't seem to mind, and I mostly did what I wanted. Although Harry didn't do drugs and was really against them from what I could tell, he did drink like a fish and was rarely sober when home. However, when he wasn't around, my mom, Richard, and I would smoke pot together on a semi-regular basis. As expected, I did not see or spend any time with my dad for most of the school year.

Kevin was pretty much the only person I hung out with in Shepherd, and occasionally we would go down to Houston. Since my dad wasn't there anymore, we'd stay with Dawn or Kevin's stepmom. One weekend when we were staying with his stepmother, we found out that a guy Kevin had recently befriended had some coke. We ended up snorting coke all night, for hours on end, with this random guy, but it was not fun sitting in his room at his parents' house. I didn't like the way the coke made me feel—paranoid and tongue-tied. For some reason though, once I got started, I couldn't stop.

As my sophomore year was coming to an end, I got caught at school with pot. Someone told a teacher I had drugs and the school expelled me. They ended up allowing me to finish my work at home so I could move on to the eleventh grade; however, they told my mother that I'd be doing so at another school. My mother's relationship with Harry had gone south and she moved back to Livingston—this time to a little one-bedroom cabin, which was all she could afford. Even if she'd had room for me, I don't think she could have taken my bad attitude and defiant behavior anymore, so she convinced my dad to let me live with him. For some reason, she seemed to think he'd be able to turn my behavior around. I was ecstatic to finally get to live with my dad and to live in a big city again. I turned sixteen at the end of the summer and my mother gave me the car she had been driving. I was going to Dallas to live with my dad and I had the freedom of a car.

My dad lived in Carrollton, a middle-class suburb of Dallas, and I started my junior year at Newman Smith High School. Newman Smith had four thousand students, which was more than the total population of Shepherd where we lived with Harry. I immediately felt overwhelmed and insignificant. At lunch on my first day, I didn't have anyone to sit with, so I went and sat at a table next to the wall. I sat on top of the table instead of taking a chair, looking out toward the entire lunch room. As usual, my way of coping was not to hide, but to get attention, which was odd since I was completely insecure. It worked. A guy walked up, said he liked the seat I'd chosen, and asked me my name. I told him my name was Deke, because I'd decided I wanted a whole new persona for my life in Dallas. I chose the name Deke because I had met a guy in Houston named Deke and I thought he was really cool. I also desperately wanted to be anyone but who I was. The guy's name was Jason, and as it turned out, he lived in my neighborhood. We ate lunch together and exchanged phone numbers.

I was anxious to find people I could hook up with to get drugs in Dallas, so I kept my eyes peeled for people who looked like they did them. In my afternoon class, I saw a guy with long red hair who had that look. His name was Ringo and I soon found out that my profiling was accurate. He did smoke pot. All I did was catch him in the hall after class and ask if he could score some pot for me. He uttered a simple yes, and that was it. We then quietly made plans. After school, we went to his friend's apartment, got the weed, and then we drove around in my car and got stoned together. Ringo and I hit it off immediately. Of course, the fact that we both did drugs was an instant connection.

When I got home, I didn't have anything to do and I didn't want to be alone, so I called Jason to see if he wanted to hang out. He met me a little while later at the neighborhood park with his best friend, Ray. I asked if they smoked pot and they said yes, so we went to a place in the woods by my house to get stoned. The spot was on a little cliff with some vines hanging down the side. They both scaled up the cliff, which was about fifteen feet high, and then told me to come up after them. As I got near the top, they started kicking dirt down on me, trying to make me fall. I continued to fight my way up, scared, but pissed off, too. When I got to the top, they said that it had been a test to see if I was going to give up and wimp out. Since I didn't, they decided I was okay to hang out with. I guess it was some sort of goofy initiation into their little two-person club. I didn't stay pissed long, though, because we all hung out and got high, and I felt pretty good about the fact that I already had three friends in Dallas. Out of this group of guys, I was the only one with a car, so I started picking them up for school every morning. Jason and Ray introduced me to another guy in the neighborhood, Paul, and I started picking him up, too. At least once a week, we would all skip school and goof off all day.

My dad and his girlfriend Gail were constantly working, and as long as I made it home by nine or ten on school nights, they didn't really bother me. I was working part-time at a CiCi's Pizza, so they could always assume I was there if they wanted to. They usually came home at about six or seven in the evening and stayed in their room until morning. I would hang out in the living room and watch TV until I felt like going to bed. Once in a while, we ate dinner together, but we usually tried to avoid having any interaction with each other. My dad and Gail were still doing coke a lot and sometimes I would sneak into their closet and steal from their stash.

Ringo introduced me to something called "car hopping," which he'd been doing for a while. It consisted of going out at night and stealing radar detectors and other valuable stuff from people's cars. Car hopping was how Ringo financed his drug habit, and pretty soon we were all doing it. Ringo knew a meth dealer named Julie who would either buy the stuff from us or give us speed in exchange for whatever we'd taken.

The first time I tried it, I was scared, but excited, too. Ringo and I drove around some upper-class neighborhoods, looking for unlocked cars or cars parked in a place where we could easily work on them for a while without being seen. The first one I broke into was a really nice Lincoln Continental—the kind of car rich grandpas drive. I used a wire hanger to jimmy the lock like Ringo had shown me, grabbed the radar detector from the dash, and took off. Soon we were sneaking out two or three times a week and car hopping all night, and then trading the stuff for meth.

It was the first time I'd taken methamphetamines (the stuff we got from Julie was a nasty drug made in someone's bathtub) and the drug would keep me awake for days. We would all snort or smoke it several days a week and go to nightclubs on the weekends to get ecstasy and acid. I still had my dream of being a dealer like Jay, the king of the club scene, but for now I was buying more than I was dealing.

Eventually, Julie started offering us coke instead of crystal for the stuff we stole. We took it, of course, and began snorting coke all the time. One thing led to another and we all began skipping school more and more often so that we could get high during the day. Sometimes I'd drive the guys to school, but then we'd come back home after our parents left for work and just sleep all day, since we'd been out all night. Nobody would have guessed that a bunch of suburban kids like us were stealing and getting high eight days a week. They say birds of a feather flock together, and I guess I had finally found people who had as insatiable an appetite for drugs as I did. We were all equally out of control.

On some weekends, we went to a place where they had illegal street racing. Everyone would line up along the road and watch cars drag race. This was a gathering of hundreds of people, all druggies—kind of like a miniature, white-trash Woodstock. There were constant fights and occasional car wrecks that kept us entertained, and it was a great place to deal drugs. In fact, this was where I started getting back into dealing.

At first, I mainly dealt acid. We would walk through the crowds, saying "trip, trip, trip," which was a way of announcing we had acid for sale—kind of the druggie equivalent of the guy at a ball game shouting "cold beer, cold beer." One night, I had the notion to cross the road—I don't remember why—in the middle of a race. I knew the cars were speeding toward me, but I just wasn't worried about it. I was high on acid and for some reason I just stopped in the middle of the road and stood there, watching the bright yellow headlights grow bigger and bigger as they raced toward me. At the last minute, Jason pulled me over to the edge of the road, and the cars blew past us. If he hadn't done that, I most certainly would have been killed, but at the time, we all had a good laugh.

We were always putting ourselves into crazy situations like that. For instance, we were also into a little game called "car surfing," which entails riding on the top of a car, standing up like on a surfboard, and going down the highway at seventy miles an hour. We thought this was pretty hilarious—you'd think we had a death wish or something.

One afternoon, we were working out at a gym that one of our friend's parents owned and we met a couple of cute girls. After a little flirting, they invited us to a party. These girls were cheerleaders and seniors at our high school, so we were pretty pumped about the invitation. When we got to the party that night, Jason hooked up with the girl who had invited us and she introduced me to her friend Kelly. Kelly was a very attractive, curvy, preppy-looking brunette. I hadn't really hit it off with girls much until then because I was always stoned and felt awkward around them. I had not had any real girlfriends or been intimate with anyone in two years, since my two nights with Shannon.

I took some ecstasy that night, which boosted my confidence. When I was on ecstasy, I felt like I could conquer the world; all my awkwardness and insecurities vanished, at least for a while, and I felt like the coolest guy in the room. I offered some to Kelly, who was all for it. Kelly and I hung out for a while, talking and making out. After leaving the party, we went to her friend's apartment and slept together. It was the beginning of a relationship with my first real love.

At home, things were getting crazier because I was getting in trouble for skipping school and sneaking out at night. I had also been stealing more and more from my parents to support my drug habit. When we moved to Dallas, the new house was smaller and a lot of paintings and accessories from the old house had to be put in the attic. I began using the attic as my personal store to take stuff from, which I would then trade for drugs. It took a long time for my parents to catch on to what was happening, and by then, the attic was half empty. The final straw came when I stole a diamond ring that my father had given to Gail as a sort of pseudo wedding ring. They knew I had stolen it. They confronted me, and I of course denied it, but Gail finally put her foot down, and said, "Either he goes, or I do." My dad kicked me out of the house, but said he'd leave thirty dollars in an envelope on the front door every day so I could get dinner and a hotel room. For a while, I stayed in a twenty-dollar-a-night dump by the freeway and ate fast food every night, but pretty soon I started staying with Jason (he would sneak me in). I used the money dad left me to buy drugs.

Since I no longer had anyone to be accountable to, I skipped school several days a week. One day, my dad told me that he and Gail were going out of town for a few days and that we'd figure out permanent living arrangements when they got back. They left on a Friday, and I decided to break into the house that night, so that I'd have somewhere to stay while they were gone. A bunch of my friends came over and we stayed high on coke and speed for the next twenty-four hours. By Saturday night, we ran out of drugs, and a guy named James said we should go rip off a coke dealer he knew. One of our accomplices had a sawed-off shotgun with a pistol grip at his house that we used to do the robbery. We didn't have any shells for the gun, so we decided to do the robbery with an unloaded gun. It's a good thing we did, because we could have ended up shooting someone.

We decided three of us would wear ski masks and kick in the door of the dealer's apartment. Then, the person in front would run in with the shotgun and scream at everyone inside to put their hands up. I was one of the three that went in while two others stayed in the car. As we walked up the stairs to the apartment, my heart was beating so hard I thought my chest was going to explode. I was on autopilot and all I could think about was doing whatever I needed to do to get more money for drugs.

My buddy Aaron kicked in the door, and James ran in with the gun, shouting incomprehensibly, with Aaron and me right behind him. Luckily, the dealer and a couple of his friends were all sitting in the living room getting stoned, and they just froze. James knew where the dealer kept his stash, so he told Aaron and me where to look. We ran into the bedroom and found the coke and a pile of money. It was about five hundred dollars' worth of coke and a few hundred more in cash. We then ran out of the bedroom, and James followed us out the door. We ran as fast as we could to the car and jumped in. As we were driving away, we all laughed and high-fived. The adrenaline rush was so intense that when it was over, I felt like I wanted to throw up. This was another opportunity to get ourselves killed, but somehow we all survived it, and we got enough money and coke to keep the party going for a while.

Late Sunday night, we ran out of coke and could not find any more, but we still had some cash left, and we all wanted more drugs. Aaron said we should go down to the projects and get crack; we'd heard about it on TV. We went cruising around a very dangerous neighborhood at three in the morning, assuming we'd find someone selling. We were right. This was the kind of run-down area that even the cops were scared to go to. After just a few minutes of driving, we pulled up to a corner where a black guy and a Hispanic hooker were selling dope. They obviously knew what we were doing down in that neighborhood, and when they saw us, they waved us over. The dealer told us if we gave them a ride somewhere, he'd get us high and give us some extra crack.

When he got in the car, he showed us how to smoke crack. When I took my first hit, it sent me into utter oblivion. My ears began ringing, my vision blurred, and I felt instantly wasted. The high lasted for only a few minutes, but I was immediately hooked. All I could think about was the next hit off the pipe. I was so wasted that I didn't realize how surreal my situation was: I was sitting in my car, in a dangerous neighborhood, in the middle of the night, smoking crack with a dealer and a hooker, and giving the dealer a ride to buy more drugs.

After we dropped the dealer off, Aaron and I went back to my dad's house, where all the other guys were hanging out. We all smoked the crack the dealer had given us, and before we knew it, we were well into Monday afternoon. For some reason, the other guys didn't seem to have the same cravings for crack that I did; I responded differently than the rest of them. They wanted to smoke and get high for fun, but I felt the need to smoke and get high. None of us had slept much since Thursday night and we were all pretty delirious from the drugs, booze, and lack of sleep, but we still wanted more.

Aaron came up with the bright idea of driving around the alleys behind houses in the neighborhood, looking for open garages we could steal stuff from. Somehow, we all thought this was a good idea, even though it was the middle of the day. Ringo was the only one who disagreed, but he still came along for the ride. About two garages and a set of golf clubs into this little escapade, we were stopped by the police and arrested for burglary. The arrest took place in the middle of the street near the school, so everyone at school saw us getting cuffed and being forced to lie facedown on the hot pavement.

We were taken to the police station and booked, but we all explained to the police that Ringo hadn't been involved in the stealing, so he was released. Jason, Ray, Aaron, and I all went to juvenile detention for burglary. My dad was still out of town, so I had to call my mother in Livingston to come get me out of juvie. It took her a few days to arrange to get off work and drive up to Dallas, so I spent that time in a cell, wearing an orange jumpsuit and feeling sorry for myself. The place was basically a jail for juvenile delinquents, which of course is exactly what I'd become.

I was relieved when my mom finally got there, although I was a little nervous about how she would react. Basically, she didn't. She just gave me the silent treatment, which I guess is the best I could've hoped for. When she got me out, we went to my dad's house and discovered that everything of value had been stolen. When I walked in, I couldn't believe what had happened, and I knew it was going to be over with my dad and Gail. I was pretty sure James and his friends were the culprits, and that they had done the job while we were stuck in juvie.

Mom tried calling my dad, but couldn't reach him. She took me to stay with her until Dad returned, at which point they'd figure out what to do with me. He arrived home a few days later and discovered that his home had been broken into, and everything worth anything had been stolen. He was furious and decided that this was the last straw, and that there was no chance of me living with them again. He decided he would get me an apartment and he would alternate between staying with me and staying with Gail. So, I moved into a pretty nice one-bedroom apartment in a decent neighborhood. Needless to say, the original arrangement of my dad bouncing back and forth didn't happen, and soon I was a sixteen-year-old drug addict, living alone in an apartment where someone else paid the bills. This was just fine with me, because I could do whatever I pleased, whenever I pleased.

I was convicted on the burglary charge, but I got off pretty easy. My sentence included some light community service (I had to clean a fire station for two hours a week), and I also had to report to a probation officer once a month for a year. I was relieved that my run-in with the law had not had more dire consequences, but things were not okay by any stretch of the imagination. In addition to my legal problems, I was also having trouble at school. It was not long before the school principal called me into his office to let me know that the three-quarters of my junior year that I'd completed so far wouldn't count, because I had too many unexcused absences. This meant that I'd have to repeat the eleventh grade. The school also decided to expel me for the rest of the year, since I'd have to start over in the fall anyway. I informed my dad about the school's decision, and he really didn't seem to care. I guess I didn't either.

The school told me about an alternative school called Valley View, where you went half days and worked at your own pace. If I went to this school for delinquents and caught up on all of my work, there was a chance I could get credit for the eleventh grade and move on to the twelfth. Of course it would require discipline on my part, and being a sixteen-year-old drug addict with virtually no parental supervision, discipline was something I didn't have a lot of experience with. I went for a few weeks, and then got kicked out of that school as well.

Around this time, my dad informed me that he was moving to North Carolina and that I was not invited. He said, however, that if I got my GED and enrolled in a community college, he would continue to pay for the apartment and utilities, and would also provide a small food and gas allowance. I looked at this as a great opportunity to continue doing whatever I wanted. All I had to do was go take a couple of classes and convince him I was doing what I needed to do. Since he would be in another state and was completely self-absorbed anyway, this seemed pretty easy to me.

While all of this was happening, my friends Jason and Ray had been shipped off to drug treatment centers due to our arrest. Ringo and Paul were still in high school, and Aaron was sent to New York to stay with relatives. I was hanging out with various people, but no close friends.

I decided to focus on dealing drugs for extra money, but I resolved not to do coke or crack anymore, since that led to stealing. The whole juvie thing had really freaked me out and I didn't want a repeat performance. I figured I would just stick with ecstasy, acid, pot, and alcohol.

My relationship with Kelly continued throughout this time. She and I had been dating steadily for a few months and we were in love. I felt accepted and loved by Kelly, and it was one of the first times I felt safe with anyone. It really helped my self-esteem to have someone love me and not take advantage of me in any way. We had fun together and she gave me a sense of security.

Kelly graduated from high school and moved in with me soon after. When Ray got out of treatment, he lived in the apartment for a little while and fell back into his old life. When Jason got out of treatment, he continued to hang out with us, but he had quit drinking and doing drugs. The rest of us partied like usual and he just tagged along. This was a really fun time for me. Things were slightly less crazy and we went to concerts and clubs; we had fun partying. I was dealing a lot of X and pot, which kept me flush with cash and gave us money to go out all the time. My using had increased to the point where I was taking twelve or thirteen hits of X a night, while everyone else was wasted on one. I had been taking so much for so long, that I had to eat three or four pills at a time just to get a buzz.

I was taking a couple of college classes and becoming a pretty successful dealer. In fact, I was even selling pot to my English professor, which gave me enough leverage to not do any work in that class and still get an A. I became reacquainted with some people I knew in Houston and I flew out there once a week to make transactions. I also had customers in Lubbock, so my traveling and drug dealing quickly got in the way of going to school, and I decided to drop out after a year. My dad stopped supporting me after that, so I got all of my income from dealing.

Despite Dad's withdrawal of financial support, I was able to live comfortably. Kelly worked as a bartender and we shared all of our living costs. I was bored though, and after a while I felt like I needed to do something with my time, so I started working at a tanning salon as a part-time salesperson. It was a pretty laid-back environment and I could deal drugs from the salon. I had a knack for sales, though, and it wasn't long before I was making good money on commissions.

Everything was going along smoothly and one day I got a call from my old friend Mitch. He was going to school in Boulder, Colorado, and said there was a great opportunity to sell ecstasy and pot there if I was interested. I decided to take a hundred hits of X and a pound of pot to Colorado by plane. I taped the ecstasy tablets and the pot all over my body. I put the pot in one-ounce bags and put each of those inside another bag filled with coffee; I was worried about the smell of the pot and figured the coffee grounds would help mask it. I was terrified the whole way through the airport and during the entire flight. I was sweating bullets, expecting to get busted. Amazingly, I ended up making it to Colorado just fine, and Mitch and I proceeded to sell the whole lot over the weekend. I made a substantial amount of cash on that deal and had fun partying in Boulder.

While I was there, we went to a bar, and I ended up getting wasted and fooling around with a girl I met. I had never cheated on a girlfriend before and I felt horrible about what I'd done. I truly was in love with Kelly, and when I got home, I immediately confessed. She looked shocked and hurt for a moment, but then became simply furious and blurted out that she had also been unfaithful, with a co-worker. We had a huge fight, and she moved out of the apartment that same day. Initially, I was totally devastated, full of shame and guilt for my actions. This was soon replaced with feelings of anger and betrayal, though, and I was left feeling more alone than I had in years.

With Kelly gone, there was nothing left for me in Dallas. My dad was gone, Jason wasn't around much anymore, Ringo was in jail, Paul had moved to Florida, and Ray had moved to California—I didn't have anybody or anything to stay for. I felt so alone and disconnected. My communication with my family was nonexistent, and the one person I had allowed myself to get close to, and even fall in love with, was now gone. I was getting tired of the life of dealing and using. Deep down, I knew I was wasting my life, but I just didn't know how to break the cycle; I had been living this life for a long time. I decided I needed to get away from Dallas and make a fresh start, so I moved back to Houston.

CHAPTER 3

This time when I moved back to Houston, I lived in a nice apartment and got a full-time job as the assistant manager in a tanning salon off Richmond Avenue, right in the middle of the party area of town. I was a natural at sales and customer service, and I was fairly reliable, so within a few weeks, I was promoted to manager. I was also having a great time dating casually—and doing a lot of it—after getting out of my two-year relationship with Kelly. I was still getting drunk at various bars every night and smoking pot every day, but I had stopped dealing and part of me really wanted to try and change my lifestyle.

My old friends in Houston who had introduced me to dealing—Jay, KC, and Chris—had all been arrested in a DEA sting, and they were no longer dealing. KC and Chris were in jail, and Jay had gotten off with probation. It wasn't long before I made new contacts, though. I always positioned myself near dealers because I needed them, and it was a short step from buying to dealing. Finding drugs had always been easy for me. One of the guys I worked with at the tanning salon, William, dealt X, and I was dating a girl named Heather who tended bar at The Pig and Whistle and had a reliable coke connection. I had managed to stay away from coke for almost two years, but once I started dating Heather I began snorting it again. Just as it always had done, the coke grabbed ahold of me and became a regular part of my drug and alcohol regime. The easy in I had with William and Heather's connection was too good to pass up, and soon I was making deals again. I was still on my mission to be like Jay and the rest of the guys, but without the jail part. I was convinced I would never be dumb enough to get busted, and before long I was dealing heavily and making good money. I had grown my dirty-blond hair long, there were plenty of girls around, and people knew me at all the clubs. I felt like I had finally arrived and I was just like Jay had been years earlier, when he first introduced me to dealing.

One night, Heather and I were driving around with an ounce of coke, several bottles of liquor, and a 9-mm handgun in the car, when we got pulled over at a random drunk stop (or maybe not too random, since we *were* drunk). Being pulled over went a long way toward sobering me up, though, because I knew I was in big trouble. The minimum sentence I'd face with that much coke and a firearm in my possession was twenty years, and they had me dead to rights. The young cop approached the window with his flashlight shining toward us and a stern expression on his face. But when he shined his light in the driver's side window and saw Heather, he just smiled and shook his head. It turned out he was a friend of hers, an off-duty patrolman at the bar she worked at, and he backed up and

70

waved us through. I was numb with relief. In that moment, I had seen my whole life go down the tubes. Twenty years in the state penitentiary would have been like a death sentence. After we made it through the ordeal, we couldn't believe our luck and laughed about how close we had come to getting busted. It was way too scary to take seriously.

Within a few months of returning to Houston, I was back into dealing heavily. I liked the freedom money brought and I knew I had to work with larger quantities of dope in order to make real money. Most everyone in the scene knew who the big player was, but he was extremely hard to get connected to. His name was Carlos, and he was big time. I would see him around at the clubs he owned, but nobody I dealt with was connected to him. After Heather and I fizzled out, I started dating a topless dancer named Jenny, whom I had met at a night club. As it turned out, Jenny knew Carlos from the club where she worked. I knew he was my ticket to the big leagues, so I talked her into introducing me to him. He agreed to meet and check me out before we got into business together.

I went to his apartment, and there were seven or eight guys there, along with Carlos and an old Hispanic lady. Needless to say, the old lady looked kind of out of place, but they treated her with a certain amount of deference. She was quite old, maybe eighty, and her hair was thin, white, and wiry. She was wearing a ratty-looking housecoat, a nightcap, and slippers. She told me to come sit by her, and I took a seat next to her on Carlos's couch. She turned to face me and took both my hands in hers. She told me to look her in the eyes, and then, in lightly accented English, she began asking me all manner of random questions—about my family, where I was raised, if I'd done well in school, if I believed in God. It was bizarre and surreal, and I didn't know what these questions had to do with anything, but I answered them. I was afraid that I'd say the wrong thing and who knows what would have happened to me then. But I didn't know what she wanted to hear, so I couldn't have lied if I wanted to. Anyway, I passed her test. She released my hands and nodded to Carlos, and he proceeded to introduce me to everyone in the room. Each of the men had a specialty, and if I needed a certain drug, I would talk to the man who handled that drug. Carlos never dealt directly with me or anyone I knew. I had finally made it. I was just like Jay. I was dealing large quantities of coke, pot, and ecstasy—more than I ever had before.

I tried to lay off coke because Jenny hated it and Carlos would not deal with anyone using it. But one night when I was delivering cocaine to a few people, they asked me if I wanted to stay and do some with them, and for some reason I said, "Aw, what the hell?" I fully intended to do just one line and then get back home to Jenny. But I could never control myself, especially when it came to coke. One line turned into a twelve-hour-long marathon coke session and I didn't arrive home until dawn, strung out and exhausted, only to find Jenny waiting up, furious with me for choosing cocaine over her. She broke up with me, and from that point on, I was back on coke full throttle.

I was pretty upset about Jenny leaving at first, but I hadn't loved her like I'd loved Kelly. We didn't see things the same way. I remember one night a stranger had gotten shot outside my apartment, and I ran out there and tried to do CPR on him. I was freaked out, bawling and pumping the guy's chest until I was winded and covered in his blood. The ambulance showed up, but there was nothing they could do; he'd been shot in the face, which I hadn't realized. I got out of the paramedics' way and looked to Jenny for comfort or sympathy, but she was completely cold about the situation and said, "People get shot and die all the time, Derek." Her callousness freaked me out, and I knew then we would never last, so our breakup wasn't as devastating to me as the one with Kelly had been.

Life went on without Jenny and I was making serious money dealing, so I quit working at the tanning salon. A friend of mine named Steven was staying with me, and he somehow got hooked up with the Vietnamese mafia. They specialized in guns and counterfeiting, and we specialized in drugs. They wanted coke, so we traded a few ounces of it for counterfeit money and went on a spending spree. I went to Dallas for a weekend to get rid of the money, and Steven stayed in town. When I returned to Houston, I found out that he had been busted by the Secret Service for passing the bills in a club and was in jail. At seven the next morning, I got a knock on my door, and since nobody I knew was ever up that early in the morning, I was sure it was the feds coming to snag me. I opened the door and there they were—I was right. Luckily, all the money I'd had was gone, and I told them that Steven was just a roommate, whom I barely knew, and that I didn't have anything to do with anything illegal. Somehow I convinced them, but, like before, I was lucky. This was another close call. If I'd gotten busted, it would have cost me years in prison—Steven was sentenced to ten.

I was snorting a lot of coke at this time, and one night my nasal passages were so messed up, I couldn't get any more up my nose. It was bleeding constantly and my sinuses were so swollen I couldn't breathe, much less snort anything. In order to continue feeding my craving, I decided to start smoking it instead, and just like that, I was back on crack. I stayed alone in my apartment, getting high on crack for two full days. My lips were dry and cracked, my eyes swollen and bloodshot, and I had blisters on my hand from flicking the lighter and holding the pipe. It was pure self-degradation; I hated myself. For two days, I sat in my apartment with the blinds closed and the phone turned off. When someone would knock at my door, I would go hide in the bathroom because I was ashamed; I didn't want anyone to see what I was up to. Plus, I didn't want to stop.

Finally, after forty-eight hours of smoking crack nonstop, I ran out. I felt completely shattered, emotionally and physically, when it was over. My head hurt and my throat was sore and I couldn't bring myself to eat anything. I was so depressed and miserable I started to seriously contemplate suicide. I couldn't understand why I kept doing this to myself. Instead of killing myself though, I went to my mother's house for a couple of days to try and get my head clear. I have no idea why I went to her house, but I guess I felt so miserable I was looking for someone to hold me and reassure me everything would be okay. Of course, I didn't tell her what I had been doing, and she didn't tell me everything would be okay. After leaving her home, I swore to myself that I would not do any more coke, but the cravings were stronger than I was, and within a few days I was snorting again.

Back in Houston again, I was contacted by my friend David, who I partied and did deals with. He was doing a scam with hot checks. He dropped by my place one night and offered me a thousand dollars' worth of X for my driver's license. He wanted to use it to forge checks he and his friends had stolen from businesses they had burglarized. I was supposed to go report my license lost at DPS the next day and we'd both be in the clear. The next day, though, I was too busy getting wasted to remember to go to DPS, so that didn't happen.

About a month and a half later, I finally went to get a new license. While I was at the counter, the lady politely asked me to wait a moment and left the room. When she came back, she was accompanied by a DPS officer who told me to come with him. I was arrested right there at the DPS office for my involvement in the scam. I truly had no idea what was going on as the officer handcuffed me and read me my rights. All he told me was that the warrant was for "forgery by passing." I had no idea what this meant, but I eventually realized it was related to the check scam my friend had been doing with my license. They searched me, and it was pure luck that I didn't have any dope on me just then.

After I sat in a holding area for about an hour, they transported me to the Harris County Jail, where I spent fifteen hours in a holding cell with hardened criminals. Some of them were there for crimes like rape and murder. I was just a scared punk kid, and I knew I was in serious trouble. When it was time for me to be processed into the main jail, I was strip-searched and given an orange jumpsuit and flip-flops. The jumpsuit was about five sizes too small and skintight and I couldn't retain my underwear because boxers weren't allowed. One of my flip-flops was broken, so I had to drag one foot. There wasn't much chance of me making any speedy getaways in this getup. Add to that my long, blond hair and there was no doubt I was going to be the belle of the ball. As I limped down to my cell with my broken flip that didn't flop, I heard cat calls and whistles and threats from the other cells. I was absolutely petrified about what was going to happen when I got to the cell block. I had no idea what jail would be like. All I could think about were the horror stories of people getting raped, beaten, and stabbed. The fear I felt walking to my cell was unlike any I had ever felt before.

They sent me up to the eleventh floor, which was known as "the gladiator floor." This was where they sent all the young guys and gangbangers. There was constant fighting between all the different individuals and groups trying to establish dominance; it was a war zone. After nearly sixteen hours of being processed, I made it to my cell in the middle of the night. I fell asleep for a couple of restless hours before being woken up by a half dozen or so inmates shouting, "White boy in the tank!" I was the only white guy on the cell block at that moment, and a bunch of the inmates were surrounding my bed and snatching the state-issued toiletries from the end of my cot. I knew I'd have to defend myself, so I picked the smallest guy—I'm not completely crazy—and shoved him. Just then, the guards started calling us for breakfast, and the whole thing broke up; I guess they were hungrier for breakfast than they were for a piece of me at the moment. But I knew it wasn't over.

After a delicious breakfast consisting of dry grits and a stale piece of toast, the guy who was kind of the leader said it was time to see what I was made of. He was in for homicide, and had "Bam Bam" tattooed on his chest. The tattoo was not related to the character from *The Flintstones* cartoon, but rather the sound his gun made as he shot people. I knew right then that my worst nightmare was about to come true. Everyone shouted, "Take it to the square!" That meant to go into one of the cells and fight so that the guards couldn't see what was happening.

The cell block had a large central common area with individual cells along each side, which is where the "living quarters" were. The inmate I was supposed to fight was a member of Bam Bam's gang. He was in for murder as well, and he outweighed me by at least fifty pounds, so needless to say, I wasn't real excited about this. I knew I had no choice, though, so I started heading for a cell, my heart pounding and sweat beading up on my lip. Just before I set foot inside the cell, a guard called my name. He said I was being transferred to Montgomery County, which is where the checks had actually been cashed. I felt so relieved to be off the gladiator floor and away from all those sociopaths that I didn't really care where I was going next. Once again, luck saved me. I narrowly avoided getting dragged into the cell and having the tar beaten out of me, or worse.

I was transported to the Montgomery County Jail, just outside of Houston, and I spent several days in a cell alone. I had never known before how slowly time could pass. I almost would've preferred to be back on the gladiator floor than to sit there alone all day and night. I hated myself too much to enjoy my own company. To make matters worse, I was also craving a drink or some dope pretty bad. I hadn't gone this long without drugs or a drink since I was eleven or twelve years old.

I used my one phone call to contact a girl I was dating, and after a few days she scraped together the money to bail me out. When I was released, I called a lawyer, and my first court date was set for a few months later. My dad had long since cut me off, but I called him up and talked him into helping me pay for a lawyer. Of course, I told him that my license had been taken by someone at my apartment, and that I didn't have any involvement. I doubt he believed me, though, because he had witnessed firsthand that I was a thief and a liar. Since his move to North Carolina, we rarely spoke, except when I called to ask for money.

When I finally got back to my apartment, I felt like everything was caving in on me. I'd had a falling-out with one of my friends over a girl—his girlfriend, who I'd fooled around with—and he called me up a few days after he had been busted with two kilos of coke. He tried to get me to do a deal with him, but I knew he was setting me up and I told him to take a hike. Desperate for cash, I had another deal going with a guy named Larry for a half kilo of coke. I picked up the half kilo from one of Carlos's guys, Reggie, and was instructed to bring the money back later that night. Because I was paranoid, I sent Larry to go meet the buyers. He was supposed to see the money before I brought the coke to the meet. The plan was for him to tell the buyers that he had the stuff in his car and see if they busted him when he went to open his trunk. If everything went well, he would tell them he didn't really have it, call me, and I would bring the coke.

Well, it turns out that these guys were cops, and when Larry went to open his trunk, they busted him. Since he didn't actually have any drugs on him, they let him go after questioning him for a few hours. While this was happening, I was having my own little coke party with the half kilo, and getting increasingly paranoid. When he was released, Larry called me and told me what happened. I just knew I was going to get busted soon. I decided to tell Reggie and Carlos that I had been driving to do the deal, saw Larry getting busted, and threw the coke out the window of my car. After hearing my story, Carlos told me to come to his place and tell him the story in person, but Reggie liked me, so he told me that if I went to Carlos's I was screwed. One of the rules for dealing with Carlos was that you did not do cocaine. I was totally strung out on coke and I knew I'd never make it out of there without getting killed or beaten to within an inch of my life. I told Carlos I'd be right over and then started packing. It was time to get out of Houston. I grabbed my bag of clothes and the half kilo and headed for Dallas. I stayed with some friends until I could find an apartment. My mother packed the things I'd left in Houston and brought them to Dallas. In less than a year, I had made a total mess of everything in Houston, and I was running away again.

I now had a half kilo of coke, pretty much free and clear. I was dealing a little, but mostly I was smoking and snorting coke all day, every day. Occasionally, I would go out to bars and hang out with people I knew, but mostly I would hole up in my apartment for days and days, getting high alone. My cocaine addiction went from being a nagging obsession that was always in the back of my mind to an all-consuming force. I had experienced the sensation of cravings for years, and it was as if my body was making decisions on its own. Part of me was saying, *I don't want to do this*, yet it felt as if I were operating on autopilot, and I kept doing it anyway. More times than I can count, I would tell myself, *No more* or *Don't get started*, and yet the next thing I knew, I was drunk or high. My mind would not stop obsessing about doing coke; it was all I could think about. The only way I could shut up the voices in my head was to do more, and more, and more. I would do coke for days until I was so delirious that I knew I had to sleep, and then I would drink like a fish to help me pass out. I was so out of it all the time that I slept on the floor; I was too strung out to even put my bed together. I would wake up in the morning thinking about coke and reach for it the minute I opened my eyes. I hated it, hated the way it made me feel, and yet it was the only thing I could think about.

My weight plummeted from 160 to 120 in just a month or two, and before long, my body was beat up from doing coke. I began to break out in hives because I was having an allergic reaction to the drug, but that didn't stop me. The compulsion became so intense that even after taking a huge hit off the crack pipe one night, dropping to the ground, and having a seizure, I got back up and tried to take a hit that big again. My body was being systematically destroyed, but I kept going until all the coke was gone. The sensation of feeling "high" and escaping in the euphoria of drugs and alcohol had stopped happening for me a long time ago. My use had become a disgusting habit that I couldn't seem to deny or stop. It was like the desire to eat or drink. I needed it to survive.

My self-hatred, coupled with fear about what the day would bring, was a driving force for me to try and numb myself the minute I woke up. I had started my day by getting high many times over the years, but now was somehow different. I woke up every day needing to get something in my system to help blot out my feelings. Pot was no longer enough. Now it became necessary to drink in order to get loaded enough to face the coming day. I would laugh to myself (to keep from crying) as I ruefully reflected that I was having "the breakfast of champions."

After about four months, when there was no more coke to deal, I had to find a way to get money. I started working at another tanning salon and did well enough to be promoted to manager again, despite being wasted all the time. Everybody in that business partied, and I sold drugs to all of them, even the owners. Every paycheck was spent immediately and my electricity was cut off regularly because I'd forget to pay the bill or find a better way to spend my money. Coke was really expensive without all my connections, and I started drinking more than ever. Every day started and ended with alcohol and a joint. Occasionally, I would score some coke or X, but mainly I just drank all the time and went to bars with people I worked with. I would still throw up from drinking occasionally, but I had developed a tolerance for alcohol and had really fallen in love with drinking. Drinking alcohol was also a more social activity that allowed me to feel a bit more normal than I did when hiding in my bathroom or closet smoking crack. This social acceptability was a way that I could justify getting drunk every day. I had hooked up with my old buddy Jason from high school, and he was back to drinking and getting high, so we hung out a lot. Things began to smooth out a little and I was holding down a job, which helped me feel a little more like I was doing okay.

It was all smoke and mirrors, though, and no matter how hard I tried to convince myself everything was going well, life for me was deteriorating rapidly and my past was catching up. My court date had been pushed out and I ended up failing a polygraph while trying to convince the court that I was not involved with the check scam. My world once again began to collapse around me, a slow but steady implosion, and somewhere in the back of my mind I knew things weren't going to end well for me.

One Friday night, I went to The Red Square with my friend Greg and two girls. I knew that Carlos owned the club, but for some reason, I just figured there was no way he'd actually be in

Dallas that night. I guess I figured my luck would continue to hold. We hadn't been there ten minutes when Greg pointed out Carlos to me. I looked up and we saw each other from across the room. I grabbed my friends and we ran for the exit. When we got outside, I looked to the left and saw Carlos's black Mercedes S500 idling in the street with the lights on. I had heard rumors from numerous people that Carlos had killed people, and I knew I was about to be killed or seriously hurt. We started walking quickly in the other direction, just as Carlos and a couple of his guys stepped out from around the corner of the building. Knowing there was no escape, I told my friends to keep walking. Carlos caught up with me and threw me up against the building. He began screaming, half in English and half in Spanish, and punching me. In the midst of the beating, I started talking as fast as I could. By some miracle, I convinced him to let me pay him back and allow me to work for him in Dallas. He calmed down and sized me up for a long minute, finally stepping forward until his face was inches from mine and said, "You only get one chance."

He ended up letting me go, but I knew I couldn't pay him back. I figured I had to get out of Dallas and make a fresh start somewhere else…again. I kept trying to run away from my problems, but the flaw in that plan was that I *was* the problem and there was no running from me. Wherever I went, there I was. Of course, I didn't acknowledge that I was the problem, because excuses, rationalizations, and denial were what kept me going. Unfortunately, they were also what kept me stuck in my addiction. If I faced reality, it would be too painful and I might have to actually do something about the problem.

I needed money to move, so I decided to rip off a guy in a drug deal a few months after my run-in with Carlos. It went all right, but after I ripped him off, I only had time to grab a few clothes and throw them in a trash bag before leaving town. I figured I could come back later and get the rest of my stuff. I didn't have a car at the time, so I asked a friend to drive me to Livingston to stay at my mom's for a few days until I could figure out my next move. Mom agreed to let me stay with her for a couple of months, just until I got on my feet, and she agreed to let me take over the payments on an old truck she had so that I could get to and from work. The first thing I did when she gave me the keys to her truck was head to a seedy part of Houston where I knew I could score some crack. I still had some of the money I had stolen from the dealer in Dallas, and when I saw someone on the street that gave me the nod, I knew I was in business.

I pulled over and asked him where I could score some rocks. He said he could score for me if I would get him high. I agreed, and off we went. We drove to a house a few blocks away where some hard-looking guys were hanging around out front. I was so nervous that these guys were just going to beat the hell out of me and take my money, but I was desperate to get high. Much to my relief, they took my money and gave me a handful of rock cocaine. The next step was getting a pipe and finding a place to smoke it. My new crackhead "friend" had a pipe and said he had somewhere we could smoke in peace. We drove another few blocks to a shack that was no bigger than fifteen feet square. We knocked on the door and a rundown-looking druggie let us in. There was a filthy, sagging bed, a ragged recliner, a single lightbulb hanging from the ceiling, and a five-gallon bucket that served as a toilet. It was the most disgusting and depressing place I had ever set foot in. Nevertheless, I plopped down on the bed and proceeded to spend the next twelve hours there, smoking crack with two complete strangers. When I finally ran out of crack, I got up and walked to my truck in the morning sunlight.

Once again, I had told myself that moving to a new environment would allow me to make a "fresh start," yet there I was…smoking crack. The self-hatred and self-loathing I felt as I was driving home was too much to bear. I cried as I drove to my mother's house and I seriously contemplated suicide. There were plenty of guns at my mother's house that I could use to take my life; I just wanted the insanity to end. However, by the time I made it home, I had decided to put off suicide—I don't think I had the courage to really go through with it anyway. I was totally strung out from being up all night, and that evening, I was supposed to start my new job. Strung out and feeling like I had been hit by a truck, I somehow managed to make it to work for training.

I started my job waiting tables at Bennigan's and waited for my court date. A few days after I had arrived at my mom's, a friend in Dallas informed me that the guy I had ripped off had gone to my apartment and taken evreything out of it. They took all my furniture, my clothes—everything. Now I had nothing left, other than the truck I was supposed to be making payments on and the few clothes I had grabbed before leaving Dallas.

As usual, I gradually started putting together deals—small at first, then bigger—and soon enough, I was back to dealing almost full-time. I quit my job at the restaurant and my mom kicked me out, so I stayed at friends' houses until I wore out my welcome and then I started living in my truck. In the meantime,

I went to court for the final verdict on the hot check bust. The judge said he would give me a deferred sentence, contingent upon me successfully passing drug tests every month, staying gainfully employed, and not breaking any laws for five years. If I failed in any one of these things, I would go to jail for five years. My judge was an ex-pro-football player and a preacher. He drilled me in the courtroom, making it clear that if I so much as smoke a cigarette, he would throw me in jail for the full sentence. This guy scared the heck out of me and I knew he was serious. I was relieved to receive the deferred adjudication, but my relief was short-lived. I knew there was simply no way I could quit doing drugs and comply with all of those conditions. It just wasn't in me. I had been getting high and drunk on a daily basis for nearly ten years and I couldn't fathom life any other way.

I was sure I was going to go to jail and all I could think about was how to get out of it. I wanted to disappear forever and leave all my problems behind. So, I fleshed out my grand plan. I was going to get some chemicals from a group of guys who claimed they could get what I needed to make X and I knew a chemist from Dallas who would come down and set up a lab. Once I had all of that in place, I was going to manufacture and sell enough of the love drug to leave the country and start over in Mexico or Jamaica. I proceeded to put my plan into action. It took a couple of months to get everything together, but finally the day arrived; it was March 13, 1993. I had already missed a drug test and a meeting with my probation officer, which meant I was in violation of my probation. I would be going to jail if this deal didn't pan out.

I had a twenty-five-pound bale of pot that a dope dealer had fronted to my buddy Manuel and me to trade for the chemicals, and the exchange for the ingredients I needed was set to occur at a warehouse downtown. I drove there alone, desperate, but hopeful. I wanted it to be over so I could get out of there. When I got to the warehouse, Manuel was there, waiting. Within a few minutes, the other guys showed up with the chemicals. When they opened up the box and showed us the bottles, I saw that one of the chemicals was the wrong kind. The chemical we needed was MDP (methylenedioxyphenyl), and they had brought MEK (methyl ethyl ketone). When I pointed this out, none too politely, the guy assured me it was an honest mistake and that they could get us what we needed right away. I knew these guys were lying. If they could have gotten the right chemicals, they would have brought them. It was over for me. My deal was going down the tubes and there was no way I would be able to get enough money to leave the country.

Something happened to me in the midst of this deal and suddenly I was only half aware of the guys around me. Their voices faded into the distance, and in a moment of absolute clarity I saw my life for what it was, and I saw the future I was heading for. I got a glimpse of reality after so many years of living in a world of lies. What I saw that day was the most painful, yet wonderful gift I have ever been blessed with. I finally grasped that I was a scared, twenty-year-old alcoholic and drug addict, who had made a lot of extremely bad decisions and whose life had gone completely down the tubes. I realized in one shocking, foundation-shaking moment that the way I had been living was wrong and dangerous and stupid, and that it would never bring me the fulfillment and satisfaction I craved. My view of who I was had been so distorted for so long that I actually thought the lifestyle I had been leading was acceptable. After so many years of being around people who were immersed completely in drugs and alcohol, and the lifestyle those things engender, I thought my life was normal—at least as normal as anyone else's.

However, in that instant, the lies and rationalizations I had lived with for so long disappeared. I saw the reality of my situation and it broke my heart. When I was a little kid, I had dreamed of being respected, successful, someone people looked up to. What I had become instead was a drug addict, an alcoholic, and a high school dropout, who had abandoned everything that was fruitful or productive or good, and whose behavior had alienated nearly everyone I had ever known. In addition to all of that, I had become an actual criminal, and I was going to end up dead or in jail if I didn't change my life in a radical way. All of these revelations happened in an instant, each one rolling over the last like a wave. I looked at the guys I was doing the deal with, and I told them I was backing out and leaving. I would not be coming back.

I got in my truck and started heading toward my mother's house. I was in a kind of shock, breathing as if I'd just run a mile, feeling stunned and overwhelmed. I rolled down the window and let the wind fan my face. I drove the two hours to my mother's house, crying the whole way, and tried to figure out what I was going to do. I had no idea what to do about Carlos, about violating my probation, about my living situation. But I knew that first and foremost, I had to stop drinking and doing drugs. Then, I had to figure out a completely new way to live. What I did not know was how to go about making these monumental changes.

The weird thing is, even though I knew all of my problems could be traced to my addictions, I didn't want to give them up—I knew I needed to, would probably have to, but I didn't *want* to. Nor could I even comprehend life without drugs and alcohol. I still thought that people who worked regular nine-to-five jobs were clueless and I continued to want the sense of power and separateness that dealing gave me. As I tried to get my mind around the thought of quitting drugs and alcohol, I couldn't comprehend how I would have fun, how I would make friends, how I would deal with everyday life situations. Who would I be? Up until that moment, my whole identity had been centered in being a drug dealer and user. I loathed who and what I had become, but I didn't know any other way to live. The thought of change was terrifying.

When I arrived at my mom's house, both Dawn and my mother were there. My mom was still smoking pot and drinking as usual. Dawn had by this time been married and divorced. She had stopped doing drugs a year before she became pregnant with her first daughter, and she'd remained clean, other than drinking occasionally. After her divorce, she and her two young children had moved into my mom's tiny cabin, so it was pretty close quarters. Dawn was working retail, like our mom. Even though she had managed to get the "normal" life I had decided to aim for, I didn't envy her. I didn't want what she had; I didn't even admire her. I was in some kind of weird limbo state wherein I wanted to continue to live the life I was living—the only life I'd ever known—but without the consequences.

They could see that I was a mess and I sat them both down and told them, without preamble, that I was hopelessly addicted to drugs and alcohol and that I needed help trying to quit. I needed to turn my life around. My mother called my father and they conferred in private for a little while. Then my mom came back and told me their suggestion. I was to cut my hair and get a job. *Wow, why didn't I think of that?* It was so frustrating that they thought the solution to my problems was a job and a haircut. Once again, it was evident that they were completely clueless. They thought that external changes would solve my internal issues. My sister heard what I was saying, though, and she understood what I needed. She told me that there was help out there, and that we would find it. A number of years earlier, she had dated a guy who had been sober and had gone to AA meetings. She remembered him talking about treatment centers and the twelve-step program. Luckily, she was there for me that day and helped me figure out where to go.

The following day, after a restless night's sleep and several breakfast beers, I sat down with Dawn and we scoured the phone book for drug and alcohol treatment centers to call. Since I didn't have any insurance and had been living in my truck for over a month, I was considered indigent, and there was a state-funded treatment center that would take me in and help me. The facility that I was going to required that I be at their center by six thirty in the morning, and if there was a bed available when I arrived, I would be admitted. If not, I was to show up every morning until a spot opened up.

I continued to drink and smoke pot while waiting to be admitted to the treatment center. We had to wait forty-eight hours before we could go, and on the night before I planned to show up, I convinced my old friend, Mitch, into taking me out to a bar for my last binge. We went to a seedy little bar near Mitch's house and I tried hard to drink myself into oblivion.

It didn't happen. I became drunk and miserable, but I never got the "high" effect I was looking for. It was a horrible night and the emotional pain I had been trying to numb by using drugs and alcohol, came out in full force and wouldn't go away. Drinking and doing drugs were no longer fun and had ceased to provide me the escape I desired.

Dawn and I had stayed in Houston that night at a motel close to the treatment center and she woke me up at five thirty the next morning. I had only gotten about an hour of sleep and the hangover was horrible. The emotional and physical pain was a fitting sensation; it epitomized what my life had felt like for a long time. We drove to the treatment center in silence. There wasn't really anything to say and I was saving my energy for whatever might lie ahead. The facility we were heading to was an old hospital in one of the worst neighborhoods in Houston, and it was in no way appealing or inviting. It was a fairly big building that had probably once been white, and was surrounded by a big chain-link fence with strands of barbwire along the top. The program was voluntary—the barbwire was not intended to keep the patients in, but to keep the local criminal element out.

When Dawn came to a stop, I stared at my shoes for a moment, but only a moment. Then I opened the door, picked up my trash bag full of possessions, and turned to look at her, my hand on the door. I said, "When I get out of here, I'm going to be a man, and I will be completely different." She smiled, her expression unreadable. I couldn't tell if she believed in me or pitied me, and I didn't know which would be harder to take at that moment. She said, "Good luck, and call me if you don't get in." I closed the door with finality. She waved and drove away.

I stood there for a minute. My truck had been repossessed, I had no money or real friends, and everything I owned fit into a single trash bag. Despite these setbacks, I was determined to succeed here. It was March 17, 1993—the single most important day of my life. I was twenty years old and about to start learning how to live all over again. I walked into the building, as fast as my hangover would allow.

PART 2

CHAPTER 4

Luckily, there was an available bed, so I got into the facility on my first try. The entry processing began with a bunch of questions about my drug and alcohol use, and about my financial and living status. Since I was homeless, unemployed, and had no insurance, I qualified for their free thirty-day treatment program, and based on my level of drug and alcohol use, they decided I'd need to begin with a stay at the detox center. The detox program was also state-funded and would last for ten days. After successful completion of that program, I would return to the treatment center.

As soon as we finished the paperwork, I was taken to the nearby detox center in a white van. The center looked a lot like the treatment facility from the outside: extremely depressing and a little bit scary. A chain-link fence ran around the perimeter, with a small courtyard in front and a basketball area in back with a hoop that had no net. The dorm I was to stay in had about thirty adult males in one large room and we all slept on army surplus cots; it was a lot like a homeless shelter. There were men from all walks of life there: different ages, races, religions, and socioeconomic backgrounds. Alcoholism and drug addiction are equal opportunity afflictions.

I didn't know what detox entailed exactly. Would they medicate us, strap us down so we couldn't get away, hold our hands and pray for us? As it turned out, they didn't do any of those things. Our time was basically our own; all they did was supply a place where we had no access to drugs and could come down off whatever weird trip we might be on without hurting anyone. The heavy drinkers and the heroin users were in a lot of pain and very physically ill. If they got too bad, they were sent to the hospital. People like me, who mainly used cocaine, alcohol, and weed, mostly suffered from psychological withdrawal. The compulsion to drink or use drugs didn't go away just because I wasn't actively using. I only had minor physical symptoms, though, and they consisted mostly of extreme fatigue and lethargy the likes of which I'd never known before. I rarely got off my cot and spent so much time staring up at the ugly, water-stained ceiling that I knew every inch of it, every crack in every ridge of plaster. Every waking moment, I would either obsessively think about getting high or drunk, or I would try and figure out how in the world I was going to live without drugs and alcohol. However, in the back of my mind I knew I had to figure out how to make it through this. I knew continuing to live the way I had been living would be worse than living sober.

During those first ten days, I met a couple of guys who had been in treatment before, and they tried to explain what the process would be like. The first thing they told me was that

I needed to find some sort of higher power, or God, as they put it. They said I needed to have a God that I could ask for strength to make it through this war I was waging. I had only gone to church once in my entire life; I had no true concept of God and only a basic understanding of Christianity. It's not that I didn't believe there was *something* out there; it's just that it had never been a part of my day-to-day existence. Besides, when drugs and alcohol were in my life, there was no room for anything else.

Still, I was desperate and willing to try almost anything that would help. I figured I had nothing to lose—worst-case scenario, I was talking to myself. So I began to pray silently to a God that I didn't really believe in. I asked for help staying sober and turning my life around. I felt foolish, but I figured I'd give the whole "fake it till you make it" thing a try.

To help myself, I listened to suggestions from my fellow addicts. A guy that I had grown fond of told me I should go pray with the pastor there and ask God to come into my life. In other words, I should "get saved." I felt foolish, and I was doubtful about Christianity, but once again I decided it couldn't hurt. So, I met with the pastor in his office and we prayed together. I asked for forgiveness of my sins and I professed my belief in Jesus. I was skeptical as I was saying these things and I didn't really believe, but some small voice told me to let go and follow this path. After the prayer concluded, I returned to my bed with jumbled thoughts. Hope, doubt, and confusion all mixed together in my heart and I felt uneasy. One clear feeling I had, though, was that I was much more than lucky. The fact that I had survived so many close calls with death and long term imprisonment was something larger than luck. I wasn't yet ready to fully acknowledge what was really happening, but I was aware of something going on around me and inside of me.

The ten days at the detox center seemed to last for an eternity. I lay around all day long and couldn't sleep at night. Occasionally, I'd go for a short walk around the small courtyard and try to figure out what I would do with my life if I managed to stay clean and didn't go to jail. My legal situation was still preying on my mind, but there was nothing I could do right then and there. I just had to sit out the process and hope I could straighten things out later.

During my stay, I met some people who had stories just as insane as mine, people who had done ridiculous things for drugs and alcohol, or because of drugs and alcohol. One guy, a musician, had played with Ike and Tina Turner, and boy, did he have some interesting stories to tell about touring the country and playing music. Another guy was a mortician who used to smoke crack all night while he prepared dead people for funerals. His stories of talking to the corpses and having hallucinations of them sitting up and looking at him were both hilarious and macabre. Telling war stories was about all we could do to pass the time, but it helped me realize I wasn't unique in my addiction.

When my ten days were up, they shipped me back to the treatment facility. I was assigned to a room with just one other person, which was like heaven after the crowded dorm I'd just left. It was a small room with nothing but a set of bunk beds and a desk. There was also a tiny bathroom with a shower. My roommate was a man named Beau; he was about forty and worked on offshore drilling rigs. This was Beau's second or third time in treatment and he treated me like a friend and protégé. I think that because I was young and this was my first time trying to clean up, and since he had such a hard time getting sober, he really wanted to see me succeed.

Unlike the detox center, where there were no distractions, days at the treatment center were very full. There were therapy sessions, both group and individual, and introductory twelve-step AA meetings where they tried to teach us about the nature of addiction and helped us examine the causes of our drug and alcohol dependencies. I was still in a fog a lot of the time, as my mind and body tried to adjust to operating without chemicals; for the first few days, everything seemed to be happening around me in a blur. Most of what they said was completely foreign to me. As my body and mind were adjusting to a drug-free state, I struggled to focus and think clearly; I didn't retain much of the information they presented. However, one thing they told me on the first day was clear; they said only a few of the fifty or so of us there would stay sober. Thinking back on it, quite a few people seemed to be there mostly for the three square meals and a place to sleep, but at the time, that shocked me into fresh resolution; I was determined to be one of the few who succeeded.

In addition to AA meetings and therapy, they also offered basic life skills classes, such as job training and readiness, anger management, and coping techniques. I attended some of everything. Much of it was basic stuff, like filling out job applications and preparing for interviews. However, the life skills classes, like anger management, were really helpful. I had never dealt with feelings and situations by processing what was happening and figuring out how to respond, as opposed to just reacting. I also had never learned how to look beneath my anger for the reasons

I reacted. They taught us that anger is merely a cover emotion for fear. Fear of what I may get, or not get. Fear of what someone may think of me, or not think of me. Looking deep into myself and knowing how to handle emotions and situations were not skills I had ever learned prior to that.

For recreation, we would play volleyball or basketball in the courtyard area. This was a great way to break the monotony and get a little exercise. My body was so run-down from all the chemicals and the lack of physical activity, that it felt good to move around and sweat from physical exertion. It also gave me a chance to connect with people and have fun doing something other than partying. I had been fairly athletic as a young child, playing football, swimming, and skateboarding. With the progression of my drug use, I had pretty much stopped playing all sports by the age of fourteen, and I was now able to reconnect to the pleasure these things gave me.

Thankfully, I stayed busy and the time went by quickly. It got easier and easier to make it through each day without getting high or drunk. Whenever I would start to think about getting high, I would say a prayer and ask for the obsession to be removed. Sometimes I would have to repeat my prayer two or three times, but eventually the cravings would pass. It also helped that I was in a structured environment, with a lot of support. As added incentive, I knew that even if I did suddenly decide to give up and go get drunk or high, it would be difficult. I had no money, no transportation, and nowhere to go. My options were pretty limited at that point.

When I was about ten days away from completing the thirty-day program, the counselors suggested I begin interviewing at halfway houses to continue my treatment after completing the program. Since I had no income and no place to live, I figured that was a good idea. Besides, I knew I wasn't ready to try my sobriety in the real world yet. I agreed to begin interviewing to see if I could find a place. I had heard of one in particular called A Better Way that was supposed to be the best, but I had also heard they required a one-year commitment, which seemed interminable; I had never stuck with anything that long. However, I figured I might as well go to the best place possible, and I knew that staying was voluntary, so I could always leave if it didn't work out.

Shortly thereafter, a staff member from the treatment center took me to A Better Way and dropped me off for my interview with the director of the facility. When I walked up to the front gates, I was pleasantly surprised by the beautiful landscaping and the sense of serenity that impressed me the moment I entered the courtyard. Everything was clean and freshly painted; there were huge old oak trees on one side of the lawn. This place was nothing like the treatment center, and I felt an instant sense of relief, though I hadn't even realized I'd been worried. I interviewed with the director, Victor, and he told me, "You give me 100 percent for the next twelve months, and you will one day have a life better than you've ever dreamed of." He also told me his program was one of the hardest in the state, and that it would not be a vacation. I had made the decision that I was willing to do whatever it took to make this change, and I was ready to answer any challenge that he put in front of me. I told him that I was serious about my recovery and that I wanted to come to his facility. Later that week, Victor called and told me I had been accepted and in a few more days I would be heading to A Better Way.

Several of the people I had gotten to know at the treatment center planned to go to halfway houses as well, but none of them wanted to go to A Better Way because they thought it was too long a program. Even Beau thought it was too big a commitment. I didn't understand why they wouldn't give it a shot; after all, their lives were on the line. Normally, I would have looked for the easy way out or the shortcut—I had been doing that my whole life—but this time was different. I was determined to do whatever I had to do to survive and make it out of the mess I had made of my life.

CHAPTER 5

The Texas Rehabilitation Commission offered a ninety-day funding program that would cover the cost of my aftercare program until I was able to get a job and pay my own way. I have no idea what I would have done without the help of the state-funded detox center, rehab, and now the halfway house. Jail is not a treatment solution, and what I really needed was the treatment I had been receiving and would continue to receive at A Better Way. For the first thirty days, A Better Way required that you not work, so that you would be able to attend all mandatory classes, as well as counseling sessions five days a week. After the first thirty days, I would be required to attend fewer classes, and I would then be able to look for a job. For the first ninety days, I lived in what they called "the big house." This was a set of eight dorm-style rooms with four men per room. Once I completed the first three months, I would move to one of four smaller houses for the remaining nine months.

The environment at this facility was forthright and confrontational; both the counselors and the residents called people out for any behavior that wasn't deemed acceptable. Everyone was required to wake up at 6:30 a.m., make their beds, do various chores around the facility or its grounds, and then follow a rigorous schedule of meetings or go to work. They also required residents to attend twelve-step meetings outside the facility. There was a lot of structure and accountability, which was obviously a major adjustment for me, since there had been so little structure and accountability in my life. I had to learn how to live a life of discipline and order, and how to follow the advice and instructions of other people. Up until then, the majority of my life had been run by me, on my own terms, and that had gotten me in the mess I was in. I was forced, through my own commitment to recovery, to start growing up at the age of twenty and I felt like a child. In the process of using drugs and alcohol, I had stunted my emotional growth, because I always chose to run from life by going outside the system. If there was a situation that was difficult, or that required emotional maturity, I would run away or numb myself with drugs and alcohol, as opposed to facing situations and growing.

I got to know a lot of people who were kind, friendly, caring, and intelligent at A Better Way. I'm sure they weren't that way when they were actively in their addictions, but when they were their true selves in sobriety, they were good people to be around. Every race, age, and occupation was represented within the hundred or so people living there, both in the main house and the aftercare houses; there were lawyers, doctors, blue-collar workers, and homeless people like me. The only thing we all had in common was a dependence on drugs and alcohol and the desire to stay sober. But that was enough.

I started to get pretty close with a guy named Larry who roomed with me at the big house. He was a few years older than I was and had tried to get sober a few times before, but he had so far been unsuccessful. He was convinced that he must get sober this time or he would surely wind up dead from his addiction. He shared some stories with me about his suicide attempts that were hilarious and sad at the same time. The first time, he tried to hang himself from a tree in his yard, with a rope that was connected to a chain and hook. When he jumped off of the ladder, he swung out and the chain came loose, landing him flat on his back. As he lay there with the wind knocked out of him, the chain and hook slid off the tree branch and landed smack-dab in the center of his forehead, nearly knocking him out. He said it hurt so bad he spent the rest of the day nursing the goose egg on his forehead and blew off suicide for the day. A few months later, after growing tired of fighting his addiction, he decided to try again.

He lived out in the country, about sixty miles from Houston, where there was a dirt road that he knew nobody ever used. He figured this would be a good place for him to kill himself. He parked his pickup on the road and ran a swimming pool vacuum hose from his tail pipe to his truck window and taped it all up so the exhaust would fill the truck's interior. Then he sat there with the truck running and drank whiskey until he passed out. A few hours later, he woke up and started puking uncontrollably. His truck had overheated and stopped running. He had also left the AC on, which had mixed fresh air with the exhaust fumes and had kept him alive. He got out of the truck and along came an old woman, who picked him up and drove him home. All the while, she talked to him about God's grace.

He figured all that had to be a sign that he had to get sober and stay alive.

Hearing this story from Larry caused a light to turn on in my mind. I had experienced that same grace over and over, yet I had dismissed it as "luck." I was starting to understand that God had been looking out for me so I could fulfill my purpose, and at that moment I knew my purpose was to stay sober. Larry ended up leaving A Better Way before he finished the first ninety days, and I never heard from him again. I hope he's somewhere doing great and staying sober.

Soon after I arrived, I decided to finally contact my probation officer, after having been absent and in violation of my probation for several months. I scheduled a meeting with him, and I went in to explain my situation. I nervously blurted out that I was clean, that I was really working hard to turn my life around, and that I wasn't going to be the same person I was before. Finally, I asked that they not put me in jail for violating the conditions of my probation, and I asked him if the judge would be willing to give me a chance. He eyeballed me silently for several long moments and I could tell he was trying to gauge my sincerity. He probably heard this spiel a lot. Finally, he told me that I had to take a drug test before leaving his office that day and he directed me to another room. I figured he wanted to confirm my story about being sober, and I didn't blame him. When I got back to his office, he said that he'd see what he could do and that he'd be in touch.

I went back to the halfway house to sweat it out. Both my counselor and Victor had called my probation officer to confirm my story and plead my case. I was tense for days, extremely worried that the judge wouldn't give me a second chance, and that, aside from any other consequences, the process I was undertaking would be seriously compromised if I went to jail. After a week or so, I heard back from my probation officer; the judge had decided to give me one chance to turn things around. I was so relieved; I was also even more motivated to make this work knowing that, in time, I could put my legal problems behind me.

I had been attending twelve-step meetings outside of A Better Way, and one of the suggestions from the meetings was to get a sponsor and begin working the twelve steps. A sponsor is someone who has been through the whole process, who has worked the twelve steps and can act as a guide and a mentor. I was attending a meeting one evening and noticed an older gentleman in the group who looked like a kind and gentle person. They called on him to speak during the meeting and I enjoyed what he had to share. Physically, he reminded me of a toned-down version of Albert Einstein; he had long, bushy gray hair, and bright, aware eyes that gave him a perpetually alert expression. I decided right away that I would ask him to be my sponsor.

As soon as the meeting ended, I introduced myself to him. His name was Scott B. (in twelve-step meetings we refer to people by their first name and last initial), and at that time, he was five years sober. I asked him to be my sponsor and he agreed. He jumped in right away with instructions, telling me that, for the time being, I was to call and check in with him every day. We also planned on meeting for dinner and attending another twelve-step meeting together in a couple of days. Finally, he instructed me to read through the first three steps in the Big Book, the textbook for the twelve-step program.

When we met for dinner later that week, Scott B. asked me to tell him about my drug and alcohol use. I told him all about the escalating nature of my experiences with drugs and alcohol, starting with the first time I got drunk at the Mexican restaurant at the age of eight. I explained how I never could seem to control myself when it came to drugs and alcohol, how I would swear to myself that I was going to quit, but it never worked. I also explained to him that when I used drugs and alcohol, it was as if all of my thoughts and actions were happening on autopilot and I was just along for the ride. I admitted that even when I didn't feel like doing more, I would continue anyway, until I ran out or until I passed out, as if I were possessed. We also talked about how my drug and alcohol use had been the driving force behind my legal, financial, and relational problems.

After I had exhaustively recounted pretty much my entire history of drug and alcohol use, Scott B. asked me if I believed that I was powerless over drugs and alcohol and if I thought that my life was unmanageable. I said yes. He then proceeded to discuss another type of unmanageability completely unrelated to external issues. He told me about emotional unmanageability—things like feeling irritable, restless, discontent, fearful, and just basically uncomfortable in my own skin. I fully understood what he was describing and related that I had been feeling those things for as long as I could remember. It was as if drugs and alcohol had been my way of leveling out and managing myself emotionally. However, in my attempts to cope with these emotions, I severely overindulged and got completely out of control. Scott B. explained that what we were discussing was described in the first step of the twelve-step program. Then he told me that I had just completed this step with the admission that I was powerless over drugs and alcohol and that my life was unmanageable. This was the first and most important measure I would take toward recovery.

That first step was pretty painless. I had known those things for a while and had already admitted them to myself. Scott B. then explained that for the second step I had to be willing to believe that there was a power greater than me that could restore me to sanity; this meant that I had to acknowledge the insanity of my behavior and my drug and alcohol use, as well as acknowledge and accept that God existed. Recognizing the insanity of my behavior as it related to drugs and alcohol was something I could do with no problem. I recounted for Scott B. example after example of my irresponsible behavior over the years: the bad choices, the close calls, the drug dealing, the drunk driving, the counterfeit money, and even the armed robbery. I had risked my life and my freedom so many times that it was pretty easy to agree that I was insane and out of control. We also discussed the insanity of not wanting to get drunk or high and then doing it anyway. There were so many times that I really did not want to get wasted and yet I couldn't seem to stop myself. Scott B. explained that the definition of insanity is doing the same thing over and over again and expecting different results. That made sense, because I knew what would happen when I drank and got high, but I kept doing it, thinking, *This time will be different...this time I'll manage it.*

The other half of this step, I knew, would be a bit harder than accepting the insanity of my actions. Those actions were right there for all to see. I didn't have to rely on faith—I could just look at my court papers or where I was living to know the truth. I told Scott B. that I had tried to pray and find God, but that I still didn't fully believe that He existed. I admitted that I was struggling in this area, and that although my soul was willing, my mind wanted tangible evidence. His response was to ask me if I had enough of an open mind to believe that there was *something* out there more powerful than myself that could help me. He suggested that it could be whatever concept of God I felt comfortable with, as long as I stopped trying to run the show. He explained that I had to decide for myself what concept and understanding of God I was willing to accept, and he stressed the importance that my understanding of God should be that of a forgiving God who deeply loved me. He then explained that all that was required to move forward was that I have an open mind and be willing. I told Scott B. that I was open to the existence of God, and that I was going to continue to pursue Him. I had been praying to God and Jesus since my time in the detox center when I had been officially "saved," but I still had so much doubt about who and what I was praying to. My discussion with Scott B. that day helped me get a little closer to my faith, because it made it clear that I needed a loving God—this really hit home with me. After our talk, I had officially completed step two. So far, the program seemed relatively simple.

Scott B. then explained step three. I needed to make the decision to turn my will and my life over to the care of God as I understood Him. Uh-oh—not so simple after all. This step seemed the most complex yet, as it confronted me with God again, which was a concept I continued to be uncomfortable with. Scott B. restated that it was "God as I understand Him"— my own personal conception of a higher power. He assured me that all I had to do was make a decision to yield control of my life to this power. We agreed that my life, as run on my own will, was a mess, and that I needed a new way of living. I now understood the importance of a loving God. How could I turn my will and my life over to the care of a God who was not a loving God?

We had moved to a bench in a park area near the restaurant during our conversation, and Scott B. now indicated the time had come to recite the third-step prayer. We knelt and held hands, and he began to recite the prayer a piece at a time, so that I could repeat it: "God, I offer myself to Thee, to build with me and do with me as Thou wilt. Relieve me of the bondage of self, that I may better do Thy will. Take away my difficulties, that victory over them may bear witness, to those I would help, of Thy power, Thy love, and Thy way of life. May I do Thy will always. Amen."

When we began, I felt awkward and more than a little foolish, but after I finished saying the prayer, I felt relieved and somewhat hopeful. At the time, I didn't realize the significance of the words in the third-step prayer. It would be a long time before I really grasped the depth and power of the words we had spoken that day. Later that evening, at the end of our meeting, Scott B. told me I needed to read the section in the Big Book that explained the fourth step and that afterward we'd meet again to talk about how I was to proceed with working that step. He also told me that moving on with step four was how I would physically demonstrate the third step.

In conjunction with working the steps, I was doing the best I could to ensure my success in the program. I continued to try and pursue a relationship with God, whom I still did not fully believe in. Since the beginning of this journey, I had decided I would choose Christ and the biblical understanding of God as my concept of a higher power, and I chose for Him to be loving, understanding, compassionate, and most of all, accepting of me just the way I was. I also came to understand that God loved me too much to leave me the way I was. I also pursued honest relationships with people, and when someone I looked up to for guidance on achieving my goals suggested I do something, I did it. If I were going to gain the success I desired, I knew the best way to get where I wanted to go was to follow the suggestions of people who had what I wanted. This was a new process for me, because I had always thought I knew what was best for me. In the back of my mind, I kept telling myself that I was going to do whatever I was asked to do, and that I was going to give this new path 100 percent of my dedication for one year. At the end of the year, if things had not improved or if I was not happy with my life, I could always go back to my old life. Drugs and alcohol would always be there if I decided to turn back.

By going to twelve-step meetings, I started to meet new people and develop a network of support from people like me. We all encouraged each other and gave each other strength. We also had a common goal and a bond that helped us develop relationships. Ironically, our connection was similar to the common bond among people who drink and do drugs together, but these new relationships were based on honesty, caring, and real support. These friendships were nothing like the relationships I had always had before, which were based on greed and selfishness. In the meetings I was learning how to live life on life's terms. We would discuss situations and principles relevant to being successful in work, friendships, marriages, and every other part of life. Rarely would we talk about drinking or drugs; instead we would talk about how the steps and the principles applied to staying sober and being happy, joyous, and free.

It was amazing the kind of people that I developed friendships with at the meetings. These were some of the most successful people I had ever met. There were business owners, doctors, lawyers, and professors. You name them and they were in the meetings, walking the path alongside me. I drew so much inspiration from these men who had come from backgrounds similar to mine. They had great jobs, families, friends, and the respect of people inside and outside of the program. In short, they had created incredible lives for themselves and this gave me hope for my own future.

Two of the men I really looked up to and who I became good friends with were Dan D. and Scott W. (not my sponsor, Scott B.). Both of them had achieved sobriety at a young age and they had maintained that sobriety for over five years by the time I met them. They had great jobs, lots of friends, and a lot of fun living sober. I told myself that if they could do it, then I could do it. Thankfully, they have both remained sober to this day and continue to be role models and friends. Scott W. owns a couple of restaurants with his wife, and Dan D. is an executive with a big oil services firm. They still help out recovering alcoholics and addicts, and they live life to the fullest.

Things progressed at A Better Way, and after my initial thirty days there were complete, I began looking for a job somewhere close to the facility. I didn't have a car, so I needed something that would be within the distance of an easy bus ride. I found a job at a retail store in a mall downtown, where I worked thirty hours a week for minimum wage. In the interview, I was honest with the manager and told him about my criminal record and my sobriety. He was a devout

Christian who believed in forgiveness and second chances, and he decided to hire me. The job required me to dress in a suit, but I didn't own one. I still only had the few clothes I'd stuffed into a trash bag when I took off from Dallas the last time. Graciously, several of the guys at A Better Way loaned me clothes to wear to work each day. Needless to say, this was a humbling experience, and it taught me a lot. This time, I was borrowing clothes and accepting the charity of someone else in order to survive and make a living, not to be cool and wear clothes that would make people like me.

Life continued in this manner, and each day I struggled to do the right thing. At work, I focused on being the best employee I could be; at the halfway house, I focused on following the rules and doing what I was asked to do. In the program, I was going to meetings, praying, working the steps, and calling my sponsor, Scott B., every day. Things were not perfect, but I was putting forth a 110-percent effort to do what was asked of me. I started to exercise again for the first time in more years than I could count. Every morning, I ran three to five miles to get my day started. Taking up exercise again helped me to feel better, both physically and emotionally. For the first time in my life I felt vibrantly alert and alive, and I experienced what some people in the twelve-step program call "the pink cloud." I like to think of this as feeling and acknowledging grace and blessings. Having come so close to death and imprisonment—not to mention the spiritual death of drugs and alcohol—I was merely joyful to be experiencing a new way of life.

I had been reading about the fourth step in the Big Book, and I knew this step was going to be pretty difficult. It required that I do more than talk with my sponsor or say a prayer. The fourth step is a searching and fearless moral inventory. What that meant was that I had to do a thorough inventory of my past actions and take account of all the people I had harmed. I also had to record my present resentments and my fears. I had to write down all of the people, principles, and institutions that I was angry or resentful toward. I then had to write what happened that led me to feel angry and resentful. The final part of this step was to do a sexual inventory. This was to be done in the same format as the inventory of my resentments, and it forced me to examine how I had behaved in my sexual relationships.

I'd been procrastinating doing this step for a few weeks, but I decided it was time to get moving and stop putting it off. I remember it was a rainy Saturday morning when I decided to get started. After I wrote down each person or institution that I resented, I then wrote what had happened to stimulate this resentment and what part of me had been affected: self-esteem, pride, personal relations, etc. The final section of this fourth step was writing down what part *I* had played in the situations I was angry about. This meant I had to take accountability, wherever possible, for the situations that had angered me for so long. Some of the things I was angry about I had no real culpability in, except for allowing those situations to haunt me for so long. Others, I had to own.

Dredging up the past and thinking about all of the people who had hurt me and whom I had hurt was difficult and painful. In many ways I relived these experiences by writing about them. I was once again subject to the feelings of pain and hurt that I had been blotting out my entire life. Among the most important issues in this fourth step was my resentment toward my parents for neglecting to provide me with a healthy and loving childhood. I also had serious anger and resentment toward my mother's boyfriends and the stepfathers who had abused and mistreated Dawn and me. Writing about these and other resentments was grueling, but I asked God for strength every time I wrote, and after a few weeks the step was complete.

Once I finished writing, my sponsor set an appointment for me at his office. Since the fifth step is admitting to God, myself, *and another person* the exact nature of my wrongs, I would have to share what I had written with Scott B. Putting this stuff down on paper was hard enough, but now I actually had to tell another person about all my painful experiences and shameful secrets. Doing this was a true test of my commitment to facing my problems and changing my life.

God had placed the right person in front of me, though, by positioning Scott B. in my life. I completely trusted him and felt very close to him. In all of our interactions, he was loving and caring, and his unwavering kindness, patience, and availability enabled me to open up in this exercise. In many ways he displayed the love and attention that I had always wanted from my father. When I entered his office, we began by doing the third-step prayer again, and then I sat down in the chair opposite his desk and started reading aloud. I had written about twenty-five pages, and when I started to give an account of my life, the floodgates opened, and I began to cry. I had been carrying around this baggage for years, and getting it out in the open, in the hopes of putting it behind me, was an extremely emotional experience. As I sobbed and recounted several of my most painful experiences, I asked Scott B., "Why did they do this to me? Why did God allow this to happen to me?" He merely looked at me with love, and with the pain I was sharing with him reflected on his face and in his eyes, he said, "I love you and God loves you." It wasn't the answer I was looking for, but it gave me comfort and peace because I believed him when he said it.

By not reconciling with my past, I had allowed the experiences of my life to drive me. It was time to let that stuff go and to start fresh. It took us a few hours to go through everything, but I walked out of Scott B.'s office feeling a thousand times lighter than I had when I'd walked in. I also felt very connected to Scott B., as he now knew more about me than any other person on the planet. I was gratified that even after learning all of this information about me, he still wanted to keep working with me. I think I'd been half afraid that he would turn away in disgust upon learning the truth. On the contrary, he was able to assure me that he had done, said, and felt many of the same things I had. It was a vast relief to know that I was not an anomaly and that I was not alone.

Before I left, Scott B. told me I needed to complete steps six and seven that very day. He instructed me to go down to the chapel near his office building and ask God to remove the defects of character that I had written about. However, he said that before I asked God to do this, I had to decide if I was ready, truly ready, for God to take away these shortcomings. He explained that fear, selfishness, dishonesty, and ego had been my survival techniques for a long time, and being without them would feel different. I knew he was right—being a completely different kind of man would take some serious getting used to—but I also knew that those old survival techniques had stopped working (or had never worked), and I had to live under new principles if I wanted a new life. I told him I was ready, and then went and spent about an hour in that chapel, talking to a God I still doubted and didn't really know.

When I arrived back at the halfway house, I plopped down on my bed and fell asleep out of sheer exhaustion. I was emotionally spent and it would take a little while to feel like myself again. My time at A Better Way was passing quickly and before I knew it, I had completed my first ninety days. It was time to move into one of the smaller aftercare houses. I felt confident that I was ready for the change. I felt good about staying sober and doing the right thing.

Work was going well and before long I was the top employee at the store. My relationship with Lewis, the store manager, had grown strong over the few months I had worked there. Lewis took a real interest in helping me, both at work and on a spiritual level. He asked me if I had ever been baptized, which of course I hadn't. I grew up in a household where there were no religious activities. He then asked if I would like to come to church with him and his family that Sunday. I thought it was really nice of him to invite me into his personal life and I agreed to go.

That Sunday, I went with him and his family to church. It was odd to be in a church setting. This was only my second time to ever go to a church service and I still had a lot of reservations and questions about God and Jesus, but I was really trying to keep an open mind. All in all, it was a good experience and I told Lewis I would like to come back again. He asked if I wanted to be water baptized the following Sunday, and explained what that would do for me. He said that it was a cleansing of my sins and an offering of myself to God. He likened it to what I was doing in steps three and four—cleansing myself of the past and turning my will and life over to God. I decided to accept his offer and I was baptized the next week. Afterward, I didn't really feel different, but it did feel good to know I had done a physical act to show my commitment to this new life.

I knew I would soon need to start making more money in order to buy a vehicle and prepare for moving out on my own. I contacted the regional manager and asked what it would take to get promoted to the flagship store. I made it clear that when a position became available, I wanted the opportunity. He told me I needed to further my product knowledge, continue to be a reliable employee, and keep my sales at or above the current level. I proceeded to do the things he said were required of me to qualify for the position, and within a few months I got the promotion. With the new position my income more than tripled. This was a huge advance, and I had earned it by working hard, asking what I needed to do to succeed, and then following through.

I was soon able to buy a car and I no longer had to borrow clothes to go to work. It was amazing for me to see that when I stayed focused and did the right thing, good things happened for me. My using life had been a constant series of bad things happening because of the decisions I made and the places I put myself. Now that I was making good decisions and aligning myself with good people, I put myself in a position for good things to happen. For the first time in as long as I could remember, I was feeling hopeful and happy nearly every day. Of course, I had some days where I was a little down, but I felt grateful to be alive and free of the bondage I had been living in.

I began work on the eighth step with Scott B., wherein I was to make a list of all of the people I had harmed in any way. I had to be willing to make amends with these people and institutions. For the most part, this list came from the people and institutions I had noted in my fourth step. While working on the eighth step, I was also mentally preparing to do the ninth step. Step nine was taking the list of people I had harmed and actually making amends and setting things straight. I wrote letters to some people, and others I went and visited face-to-face. Scott B. guided me on the best way to approach each person. I wrote letters to my parents and took accountability for all the things I had stolen and all of the pain I had put them through. It was important that I only focus on the things *I* had done, without recrimination for the things that had been done to me. The task I was undertaking was about addressing *my* actions and no one else's. This step really allowed me to build my self-respect, because I no longer had to feel guilt and shame about my past behavior. I also had to stop being a victim and begin taking responsibility for my actions and emotions from this point on.

These weren't just empty confessions or the "I'm sorry" that I had used so many times in the past. I had to take accountability and ask the people I had harmed how I could make things right. I also had to make financial restitution to some of the people I had stolen from. This process did not happen overnight and it took every ounce of courage I could muster to proceed. In the end, though, I did it, and was then able to hold my head high and know that I had nothing to be ashamed of anymore. My sense of self-worth had been destroyed by the things that happened to me as a child and by the choices I had made. The steps and actions I was taking now, as an adult, were building me back up from the inside out.

One of the amends I made was to Harry, my mother's old boyfriend. I had stolen money from his wallet when I was younger, and my actions had created chaos and havoc in his home. One afternoon, while I was still living at A Better Way and was visiting with my mom at her real estate office in Livingston, Harry walked in the front door. He was on my amends list, but I had not done anything to seek him out yet. My mother was just as surprised as I was to see him. After we finished saying hello and doing a little catching up I asked Harry if he and I could step outside and talk.

My heart was racing and I was really nervous about telling him everything I had done and making amends. I started by explaining to him that I was sober and that part of turning my life around was making amends to people I had wronged. "I would like to take accountability for being disruptive and disrespectful while living with you," I said. "I am pretty sure I stole about a thousand dollars from your wallet and I would like to repay you." I pulled my checkbook out of my back pocket in order to write him a check. "Would a check for one thousand dollars be fair?" I asked. "Would that help make things right?"

"Yes, that'd be fine."

I wrote Harry a check. After I handed it to him, he looked at me with a smile and ripped it in half. Throughout this process he had kept fairly quiet, but at that moment he put his hand on my shoulder and looked deeply into my eyes. "I didn't want the money, Derek. Seeing you take accountability and be an honorable man are all the amends I needed. Good luck." He shook my hand before turning away and heading to his truck. I felt so grateful to have been acknowledged for the changed person I had become, and the sincerity with which Harry recognized my efforts touched me to my core.

The amends I made to Grandma Lyle were impactful for both of us, as well. Since getting sober, I had seen her occasionally when I visited my mother. My grandmother was still living alone in Shepherd, and she had started going to church. The people at the church had taken her under their wing and she seemed to be getting along pretty well. Her health had continued to decline as she aged—mainly due to emphysema as well as heart problems—and I felt that she might not live much longer. I had done writing in my fourth step about my resentment toward her, and in the section of the fourth step where I took accountability for *my* part, I realized I had been very hurtful toward her. I had been rude, disrespectful, and unappreciative, and I had been very callous with things I had said and done to her. These behaviors were transferred to my amends list, and I decided to write a letter to take accountability for this behavior and to acknowledge her for all the work she had done to take care of me.

I sent her the letter and waited to see if I would hear back from her. My mother called me a few days later and told me that my grandmother had received the letter and it had caused her to cry tears of joy. This phone call prompted me to get in my car the next day and drive to my grandmother's house so we could talk face-to-face. When I walked in she leaned forward in her recliner and put her arms out to give me a hug. As we were hugging each other we both began to cry. I could see my letter sitting on her end table, where she had been keeping it for several days. I told her I was truly sorry for the things I had done to her, and that I loved her. She then told me she loved me and that she was so proud of the man I was becoming. After wiping our tears we had a great talk about what was happening in her life and mine.

My grandmother passed away a couple weeks later, before I was able to see her again. My mother found her in her bed, and she told me she looked very peaceful. Despite her unkind behavior while I was growing up, I know she loved me—we were both just very hurt and wounded people who did the best we could. Knowing I had made amends and left our relationship in a place of love and care was a healing gift from God.

Through this process, I was also able to begin to rebuild my relationship with my mother and father. I made amends to both of my parents and Gail by writing letters and eventually talking face-to-face with them. By taking responsibility, I helped open the lines of communication, and we spoke on the phone regularly. My father even came to visit me at A Better Way when he was in town visiting from North Carolina. I spoke to my mother more regularly, and we were getting along fairly well. Both my mother and father had quit using drugs and had changed their lifestyles. My dad and Gail had quit coke when they moved to North Carolina, and my mother had quit smoking pot when I went into treatment. They still drank regularly, but their lives were not unmanageable like mine. It was good to know that I was not the only one in our family who was changing and growing. This adjustment in their behavior also allowed me to feel closer to them.

Together, Scott B. and I began work on steps ten, eleven, and twelve, Step ten was to take a daily inventory of my behavior. That meant that when I made a mistake, I was to immediately make amends to whomever I had harmed. If I so much as snapped at someone, I had to immediately go to that person and resolve the situation. This step helped me to establish integrity in my day-to-day life and kept me from building resentments.

Step eleven was nurturing my relationship with God on a daily basis through prayer and meditation. God was still a fairly abstract concept to me, but I was trying. And the final step, step twelve, was the process of practicing my newfound principles in all areas of my life and helping others with their recovery. These last three steps are a lifelong journey—a commitment designed to keep me focused on practicing acts of integrity, maintaining a spiritual life, and serving others.

Through my commitment to, and implementation of, the principles of the program, I gradually became a role model for new men coming into the facility. I completed the twelve steps, and before long I was sponsoring other men and helping them to recover. Supporting others and becoming the kind of person other people looked up to—for the right reasons—was incredibly fulfilling and healing. Ironically, helping others gave me the sense of fulfillment that I had sought to achieve with drugs and alcohol, but which had always eluded me.

Throughout this process, I developed close relationships with some of the men I was helping and sponsoring. A young guy named Grant K. came into A Better Way and we became close immediately. He was a lot like me and soon we were doing everything together. I tried to help him and let him know how I had been successful, but he just wasn't open to doing the work. Before long, he left and went back to using. Over the years, he would come in and out of the program and we would spend time together, but because he was never willing to work the steps, he would end up going back to his old ways. After years of this back and forth, he decided he couldn't take it anymore, and he hung himself one Christmas Eve. When I heard what had happened, I was heartbroken. I knew that it could have just as easily been me. The only difference between me and Grant K. was that I had been willing to do the work necessary to stay sober and find inner peace, and he hadn't. At the core of that "work" was the relationship I had developed with God. Grant K. was never willing to develop a relationship with God, and he never had the miraculous transformation necessary to be relieved of his obsession to get high.

On the other hand, I was inspired by the amazing success stories that I witnessed and was a part of. I sponsored a guy named Chris M. who is still sober and now works for Chuck Norris in the Kick Start program, presenting anti-drug programs in middle schools and high schools all over the country. Chris M. went from being a drug addict and alcoholic to someone who is helping thousands of kids stay off of drugs. I was able to sponsor him and be a part of his transformation.

It was truly a miracle to see other people go through the process and change physically, emotionally, and spiritually as I had. Witnessing these transformations happening all around me really helped me to further my faith and belief in God. By seeing and being a part of these miracles, I knew that I was not an anomaly, or a fluke, and that the process could work for anyone. These men were following the same spiritual path I was following, and we were all experiencing the same incredible transformation in our lives.

I was nearing the time when my twelve months at A Better Way would be complete. I had not taken a single drink or used a drug of any kind in a year's time. This was truly a miracle, because from the age of eleven until the age of twenty, I had used drugs or alcohol daily. Not only had I not used any substances during the previous year, but my desire to use them had been completely removed. Staying sober was no longer a hardship or a frightening prospect. I was completely at ease with sobriety.

One evening around this time, I was lying on my bed in the dark, thinking about God. I wanted so badly to know He was real, without any doubt, but I was still struggling with belief. Suddenly, I had an idea. I brazenly asked God to turn on the lights—literally saying, "God, turn on the lights, please." I knew this was a juvenile approach, but my faith was still very immature. I wanted undeniable and tangible proof that He existed. After a minute or two of asking—begging—God to show me he existed, I opened my eyes and waited. Needless to say, the lights did not flicker; there was no burning bush. I decided to give Him one more chance, and I asked Him again to turn on the lights to prove to me He was real. I told God that if He did not prove to me He was real, then I was done with trying to pursue Him. Once again, nothing happened. Frustrated, I got up and began to head out the door. As I was walking out of the room, I passed by a mirror and as I looked at my reflection I heard a voice in my mind say, "*You* are the miracle. *You* are the burning bush."

At that moment I realized that it was truly a miracle that the desire to drink and get high—a desire that had once been irresistible—had completely been removed from me. The fact that I had emerged from the darkness of addiction, that I had stayed sober, that I had completely rebuilt my life, my relationships, and even my personality, was irrefutable proof that God existed and that he was helping me. I also realized that this was the same God that I had been praying to and searching for since my time at the detox center. It had taken me a year of diligent seeking—as I like to say, God can move mountains, but you'd better bring a shovel—but I finally believed and the proof was in the person I had become.

Once again, God knew better than I did. He didn't flick on the light switch on the wall, but instead turned on a light in my heart that allowed me to see the undeniable miracle that I had become. I probably could have found a way to rationalize the lights flickering, but I could not deny what had happened in my own life. I knew then that God had been watching over me my entire life. All those times when I thought I had been "lucky," he was protecting me so that I could come to the point in life where I was ready and willing to accept Him and the love He had for me. Finally, with these revelations fresh in my heart and mind, my year was finished and it was time to leave the facility.

I moved into an apartment with a guy I had befriended in the program named Colin H. He had a couple more years of sobriety than I did, and it seemed like a good decision to live with someone who could support me and whom I could support in turn. We had a blast living together and goofing off. I was twenty-one years old and freer than I had ever been; it was almost like I was reliving part of the childhood I had missed out on when I was doing drugs all the time. Colin H. and I would do fun things like rollerblade downtown, go out to night clubs with sober friends (no drinking, just dancing and meeting girls), go to movies, and water-ski. None of the people from my past were around anymore—in fact, most were in jail or dead—and I had created a whole new world for myself. Life was really good for the first time I could remember. The fear and insecurity that I had lived with my whole life had been replaced with confidence and faith. Of course, there were trials and tribulations, but I was not completely overwhelmed with the selfishness, fear, and anxiety that had driven me for my entire life—I was thriving.

One afternoon, I called up the construction supply company where Colin H. was working. I asked for Colin H., and the guy who answered the phone said, "Yeah, he's here. Can I ask who's calling?"

"Yeah, it's Derek."

"Derek who?"

"Derek Steele."

"Oh really?" he said in an odd tone.

"Yeah."

"Okay, hold on." I definitely thought it was kind of an odd exchange, but soon Colin H. came to the phone, and I forgot all about it for the time being.

When Colin H. got home later that day, he came in looking all excited and said, "Man, you're never gonna believe what I've got to tell you. You know John, that guy I work with, the one who picked up the phone? Well, he used to be one of Carlos's boys and, you know, he did some muscle work for him. Well, Carlos had told him that he had seen you in Dallas and he wanted John to go up to Dallas and get you—he had your address and everything. He said Carlos had instructed him to put you in the trunk of the car and bring you back to Houston, and he was gonna kill you. So, John started driving to Dallas and when he was halfway there, he gets a call from Carlos, who tells him to turn around and come back, because something was going down in Houston and he needed him there."

I later found out that during the time he was hunting for me, Carlos was in the middle of being busted in Houston under the RICO Act, the organized crime act that makes it possible to prosecute people for crimes they orchestrated, even if they didn't actually commit the crimes with their own hands. Carlos never directly sold drugs, but he put a framework in place and manipulated it from the top. So he got busted, and his entire entourage was rounded up by the feds during sting operations. Faced with their own daunting realities, Carlos's men began rolling over on him. That's why Carlos called John and brought him back to Houston when he was halfway to Dallas to come get me. It was a very close call and I had no idea how lucky I was until long after I had gotten sober.

Months before Colin H. related this information to me, I heard that Carlos had been busted and was serving two fifty-year sentences back-to-back, so obviously I didn't worry too much about him. I also didn't go to the same places or hang out with the same people anymore, so I really hadn't thought too much about any of his boys. Now, though, I realized that I had been just a few hours away from being grabbed, thrown in the trunk of a car, and driven back to Houston for who knows what. It was one more close call, and the knowledge of it only reaffirmed that these were not accidents or lucky chances. God had looked out for me over and over again. He had been looking out for me long before I even knew he existed.

After leaving A Better Way, I knew I still had issues I needed to resolve, so I started seeing a therapist named Mark G. to work through some of the trauma and loss that I had experienced as a child. He had been sober for a long time and was a Vietnam vet who had done two tours as a Special Forces Ranger. He had overcome so much in his own life that I knew his experience and education could benefit me.

The fact that he was ex-military didn't deter me. Unlike my mother's boyfriend Jim, Mark G. was kind, soft-spoken, loving, and spiritually grounded.

Dealing with my past was the only way I was going to be able to have continued peace and joy in my life. I had done a lot of work in the steps, but I still had some behaviors and feelings that I knew I needed to address in order to get the most out of living. Mark G. helped me go back and work through the neglect, abandonment, and abuse that had occurred during my childhood. I revisited those memories and feelings as an adult in order to process what had happened and in some cases try to understand *why* it had happened. At times, some of the exercises seemed crazy and I felt foolish, but they worked. I learned early in my recovery that having an open mind and being willing to try new things is one of the keys to success, while contempt prior to investigation leads to failure.

One of the big issues for me had always been the fact that my father was unavailable when I was growing up and had never showed any love or emotion. I had always dreamed of the type of father who took an interest in what I was doing, who would teach me things and participate in my life. My dad was just not that guy. I was also very resentful that my father had never tried to step in and save me from destroying myself with drugs and alcohol. One of the exercises that helped was to go back and feel the feelings that I had anesthetized with drugs and alcohol. I did most of this by writing about what had happened and how it felt when I was a young child. Many of my feelings were focused around thinking I was unlovable and worthless. The assumption I had made as a child was that if I were important and lovable, then I would have been protected and cared for. I had been running from everyone and everything my whole life for fear of being hurt.

After it was all on paper, I processed these feelings and assumptions with Mark G. We did some exercises wherein I would visualize my father sitting in a chair in front of me, and I would tell him what it felt like as a child to be his son and how it had affected me. As a child, I had felt powerless and unable to understand or communicate what was happening to me and how it felt. Now, as an adult, with Mark G.'s guidance I got all of these feelings and thoughts out in front of me in order to face them head-on. By doing this, I enabled myself to move beyond those feelings and find freedom from the past.

Despite my anger and disappointment, I came to understand that my father had done the best he could with what he had to work with. One of my tasks in therapy was to interview my parents to learn about their lives in order to view them as individuals and not just "Dad" and "Mom." What I learned about my father is that he came from a home where his father's pet name for him was "stupid," and the closest thing to affection he ever got from his dad was a smack on the back of the head. Nobody had ever shown my father what it meant to be a good dad. In addition to his childhood traumas, he had his own issues with drugs and alcohol that prevented him from being available and attentive. These are not excuses for bad parenting, but it was important for me to understand my father in order to forgive him. I also had to find men who could give me the love, support, and guidance my father was not capable of giving. My sponsor, Scott B., and other men I was close to helped fill that void.

I went through a similar process with my feelings about my mother. Her preference for abusive men, and her inability to protect me, had left deep scars in me and in our relationship. It was important for me, as an adult, to reevaluate our relationship. Knowing as I did how childhood can affect the decisions we make, I decided to look at my mother's past to understand why she had made the decisions she had. I discovered that she was sexually and physically abused by her stepfather repeatedly, from the age of five to the age of fifteen, and her mother, my grandma Lyle, had known and had failed to protect her. She was also beaten with water hoses and anything else her stepfather decided to grab when he was in a fit of rage.

She had developed an aversion to religion because many times after church on Sunday, her stepfather would do things to hurt her. The church had nothing to do with what happened to her, but as a child, my mother was unable to understand that. Her stepfather was a sick person operating outside of the teachings of any church or religion, and because he was adept at wearing masks to hide his horrid behavior, no one believed he was a monster. She had tried to tell people at church what was happening, but they did not believe that she was telling the truth.

After learning how horrible my mother's childhood had been, I was no longer surprised that she abused drugs and alcohol; the wonder to me was that she wasn't in an asylum. I gained a deep respect for my mother's ability to survive such intense physical and emotional trauma. My father never had the understanding or the ability to seek counseling in order to overcome his issues. Thankfully, my mother did seek help and worked with a therapist sometime after I moved to Dallas.

Learning these things about my parents helped me to forgive them and to heal, but I still had to go back and relive the past to feel the pain that I'd blocked out. I had used drugs and alcohol in order to not feel anything—to ignore the past and the present, rather than deal with it. My early survival mechanisms were control, self-centeredness, and something my therapist called "false ego." I felt that if I projected ego and confidence, I could convince people I was good enough, but I didn't really feel that confidence. In other words, I was an egomaniac with an inferiority complex. I'd learned to be selfish as a child because I felt that no one else was looking after me; I had to do it myself. All of these character traits were not giving me the results I needed out of my present life, and I wanted more.

I knew I was incredibly lucky to have the opportunity to clear away the damage from my past so that it wouldn't destroy my future. I tried to justify that blessing from God by doing as much work as I could to heal. I continued to concentrate on resolving my psychological issues in therapy until my therapist and I agreed that we were finished for the time being. All in all, it took about a year. Through the process of my recovery, I had become a person who was driven to know more about how I operate in order to become a better human being. This was a whole new concept for someone who had been a perpetual quitter and who had always run away from situations.

I learned that alcoholism is a real illness, not just a willpower problem. It's a chronic disease, meaning it never goes away, even if the alcoholic gets sober. It's also a progressive disease—it gets worse until you beat it or until it kills you. And finally, I learned that it's a disease with major genetic factors. While not all children of alcoholics grow up to abuse alcohol, there is a good deal of research showing that alcoholism, and other physical addictions, may be more likely if there is a family history of it. One of the articles I read during my recovery was a study by the National Institute on Alcohol Abuse and Alcoholism that suggests that genetics may be responsible for 50 percent of a person's vulnerability to alcoholism. And I read another large-scale study, the Collaborative Study on the Genetics of Alcoholism (COGA), which isolated a gene on chromosome 15 that they believe is connected to alcohol addiction. What I came to understand was that I was not just "weak" or someone who lacked willpower; I was afflicted with the disease of alcoholism. Not only did I have all of the environmental factors present in my life, but there was solid evidence of alcoholism in my family tree.

I have no intention of claiming that because my parents abused drugs and alcohol, it was inevitable that I was going to become an addict. I don't deny my culpability in making the decisions that led me down the road to addiction. What I have come to understand is that addiction is more than a few bad decisions—and overcoming it takes more than a haircut and a new job. Whatever the cause, addiction is an overwhelming force, a compulsion that few people are strong enough to overcome without help—the help of the program, friends, loved ones, sponsors, and, of course, God. With God's help, I had successfully navigated the first stage of my recovery. I was sober and healthy, I had friends and mentors, I had restructured my life and reconciled with my past. But living life within the safe confines of rehab and therapy was one thing; growing up and forging a new life was something else completely—something with challenges and complications I couldn't yet imagine. However, I did believe in my heart of hearts that Victor from A Better Way had been right when he told me that I could have a life better than any I had ever dreamed of.

CHAPTER 6

I had now been sober for two years, and it had been well over a year since I'd even had an urge to drink or do drugs. By some miracle, it seemed as though not just the compulsion, but also the craving to be high or drunk, had been completely removed. I was amazed to discover that I was having the best time of my life. Something I struggled with at a young age when attempting to get sober was the fear that I was never going to have any fun when I quit "partying." In actuality, I was having more fun sober than I had ever had drinking. I went out all the time and had a blast, without all the consequences of drinking and drugging. No more hangovers, arrests, fights, and, best of all, I didn't always have to look over my shoulder in fear of who might be coming after me. During my first year of sobriety, I abstained from dating and relationships to focus on me, and to do the work I needed to do for myself. Now that I had fulfilled that commitment, I was dating again, going out with friends, and having a great time.

I was still working in retail, but I had also been working weekends and occasional evenings for a guy named Doug W. who I'd met in the program. Doug W. owned and operated his own construction company. He taught me about exterior remodeling and storm damage work. There had been a big hailstorm in south Houston, and Doug W.'s company would go door-to-door and talk to people in the neighborhood, asking questions, inspecting damage, and explaining to homeowners that if their roof or siding was damaged, the insurance company would pay to replace it. My job in the beginning was canvassing. I would go door-to-door explaining who we were and what we did, and ask people if they were aware that their roofs were damaged and that the insurance company would pay to replace them. If they were interested in talking to one of the salespeople, I would get a name and a phone number and Doug W. would send a salesperson by. That was my first job with Doug W. After I received more training, I became the actual salesperson who would go in and take measurements, give quotes, and deal with the insurance adjusters. It was a great way to make extra money, and I was getting educated on the ins and outs of construction and the insurance repair business.

I had also built a friendship with a guy in the program named Charlie D. Charlie D. owned a small roofing and remodeling company, and after a big storm hit Houston, he asked if I would come work with him, knowing that I had worked at the other company with Doug W. Charlie D.'s company was small and just getting off the ground, earning about $150,000 a year in revenue. The company was run from Charlie's apartment and he had never really done much with it. He was attending the University of Houston entrepreneurship program to learn how to become an entrepreneur and grow his business. He invited me to come join him and be his vice president, and and he offered to give me 45 percent of the company profits at the end of the year, as well as pay me on every job I personally sold and managed.

It took a big leap of faith for me to leave the security of my full-time job, but the possibilities were tremendous in the business with Charlie D. I knew that with my criminal record and a GED, my employment options were limited, and I had no intention of working as a retail salesperson for the rest of my life. I was determined to be successful and create a good income for myself. I knew that the opportunity with Charlie D. could give me the ability to write my own ticket and be more in control of my future than working in retail could. I decided to take the leap, and Charlie D. and I began doing business together when I was about three years sober. Within a year, we had grown the business by leaps and bounds, bringing in more than a million dollars a year in revenue, and winning an award from the University of Houston entrepreneurship program for being the fastest-growing business of the year. We were both doing very well financially, and before long, I was managing five salespeople. It was amazing how the hard work was paying off.

My personal life continued to improve. I bought a new SUV and a ski boat with my earnings, and I went water-skiing with friends a couple times a week. I went out to clubs and parties several nights a week, but I never felt pressured to take a single drink at these places, because traveling with several sober friends made it comfortable.

Charlie D. convinced me to go on a snowboarding trip to California, which was an incredible experience. Charlie D.

was all for living life to the fullest and we had a blast. He was big into snowboarding, and I hadn't been out to the mountains since I was a kid vacationing with my family in Colorado.

My parents' old friends, Bobbi and Gerry, had a house in LA, the house in Livingston, and a house in the mountains of California at a ski resort where they lived full time. My mom stayed in contact with them. When Charlie D. and I went on the snowboarding trip together I got in touch with Bobbi and Gerry and scheduled a stay at their home. It was a free place to sleep, and I wanted to see them. I hadn't seen them since I was fourteen and had fallen for their daughter, Shannon. Charlie D. and I went out there, and though I didn't run into Shannon again, I did get reacquainted with the mountains. We spent four days snowboarding on Mammoth Mountain with Bobbi and Gerry, who, as usual, were kind, gracious, and wonderful hosts. I called them my godparents because I'd always felt a connection to them, though they didn't officially hold that title. They served as a model for me of how to maintain a successful relationship and marriage by being present, loving, kind, and available.

I discovered a huge group of people my age in Houston who were sober, responsible, and living good lives, and I cultivated friendships with many of them. The world I had lived in before sobriety was so small and limited; I went to the same bars with the same crowd every night. At the time, I thought I was having fun—at least some of the time—but my world was too small. Being sober had enabled me to meet a broader array of people and had opened up many new experiences to me. Of course, not all of the experiences were good.

After a year and a half of working with Charlie D., I discovered that he was skimming money that he and I were supposed to split. I also learned that he had been shorting other people on their pay. It was the end of our working together. Not long after I left, the company nearly went under. It broke my heart to lose my friendship with Charlie D., but there was no way I could continue to associate with him, professionally or personally, knowing that he had stolen from me and our coworkers. Charlie D. was one of the most fun-loving and funny characters I had ever met, but he had a real problem when it came to money, and it often caused him to make bad decisions. I hoped that in time he would come around and make amends so we could be friends again.

Fortunately, by this point, I had developed a reputation in the remodeling and insurance repair business as someone who was honest, hardworking, and produced good results. I decided to bank on my reputation and set up my own company. I worked out of my home, and with the help of a salesperson for one of my suppliers, was able to establish a connection with another company, Ideal Roofing and Siding. They sent me a ton of business. Ideal would fax me leads every day which I would use to generate roofing and siding sales. Once I sold a project, I would notify Ideal and schedule materials, manage the subcontractors, and collect all of the funds. Ideal would then handle all of the payments to suppliers and subs. We split the profits sixty-forty. I was in essence my own boss. This relationship worked out perfectly and allowed me plenty of freedom. I also bid projects that were 100 percent mine on the side, but Ideal kept me so busy running their leads, that I had very little time to build my own clientele.

Almost everything in my life was going well—the only thing I longed for was a relationship with the type of woman I could marry. I had been dating regularly, but the types of women I seemed to meet and go out with were not the types of women I felt I could be serious about. It seemed as if all the women I was attracting were very self-absorbed and were not women I could trust to be faithful. They were also what I would call "party girls," who spent a lot of time in bars and clubs. I went back to my therapist, Mark G., to try and figure out why I was attracting these women who were wrong for me. He suggested that I take a six-month break from dating and spend that time focusing on myself. He also suggested that I change some of my actions to start attracting a different type of woman. I needed to quit going out to bars and clubs to meet women and I needed to adjust some of my attitudes and behaviors. In the process of talking with Mark G., I realized I was dating women who were mirror images of me. I was a "party boy," who always hung out at bars and clubs, and I was the type of guy who would bounce from woman to woman with little interest in being serious or monogamous. I was also completely self-absorbed.

Mark G. and I spent some more time talking about my issues with my mother, and my distrust of women which stemmed from that. We worked to clearly define what kind of woman I wanted. Mark G. had me write a description of my ideal woman and then he asked me if I wanted to know how to get that woman. Naturally, I answered yes, and then waited for the big secret. Well, needless to say there was no big secret, and no magic formula either. He explained that I had to develop the traits I was looking for in others. In order to attract a different type of woman, I would have to change myself into a different type of man. This sounded like a logical concept—not easy, but logical—so I set about the task of figuring out what areas I needed to work on. We agreed that I would refrain from dating for six months while I integrated these traits into my life.

Being single for six months was pretty tough after months of carefree bachelorhood, but it gave me time to work some things out. I would spend time each day imagining the perfect woman, and then imagining how I could become good enough to deserve her; it was a different sort of meditation than I'd been used to, but it really helped me to see what changes would be necessary in my personality, habits, and expectations. I stopped hanging out in night clubs and chasing women all the time. For distraction, I took this time to really focus on helping men in the program work on their sobriety and recovery. I had quite a bit of extra time, since I wasn't going out five nights a week. I filled that time working with newly sober men, because I knew that I could not think myself into a better way of acting; I had to act myself into a better way of thinking. In order to stop being selfish and self-absorbed, I needed to get out of myself and go help someone else.

When the six months were finally over and I was ready to start dating again, I had dinner with Rob D., a guy I had recently befriended, and we talked about relationships. We talked about the type of woman we wanted to meet, and we agreed that we would pray and focus our energy on meeting that type of woman. We had both been through enough bad relationships to figure out what we wanted in a partner by eliminating the characteristics we didn't like. I decided to consider the unhealthy and unfulfilling relationships of my past as necessary stepping stones to prepare me for the right relationship.

One Saturday, about a week later, I was hauling my boat to Clear Lake to go water-skiing for the day. A few friends were with me, and as we were driving down the freeway, a carful of girls pulled up next to us, and we waved at each other. Judging by their clothes and the gear in their car, they were heading to the beach. They appeared to be about our age and they were all really cute, so I rolled down my window and invited them to meet us at the lake to go swimming. About half of them immediately said yes, and the others no. I just shrugged and said that if they wanted to come, they could follow us. I was really hoping they would come, because one of the girls was a pretty, blue-eyed blonde, who had caught my eye. Our exit for the lake was approaching, and when we got off the freeway, I kept my eyes in the rearview mirror to see if they would follow us. Much to my disappointment, they kept going straight. I figured they had decided to blow us off and were heading to the beach.

My buddy Chris K. had never been out on the boat with me before, and he was as pasty white as a porcelain doll. He insisted that we stop and get SPF 60 sunblock, as opposed to the SPF 15 I had in the boat. I was in a hurry to get to the water, but I stopped anyway. As we were pulling out of the store parking lot, I saw the same girls we had invited to come skiing with us driving down the road toward us. They had changed their minds and decided to turn around and look for us. I was so glad Chris K. had insisted we stop; if we hadn't, we would have missed them, and my life would be very different today.

Luckily, they spotted us pulling out of the store, and I waved at them to follow us to the boat launch. When we made it to the lake, they continued to sit in their car instead of getting out right away; the girl I thought was cutest rolled down her window and proceeded to interview me—presumably to determine whether or not I was a weirdo or an ax murderer. She asked me a series of slightly personal but very basic questions, like whether or not I was married, went to school, had a job, etc. After the girls discussed my answers, they decided I'd passed the test and they would come ski with us. It turned out that the girl I liked was named Becky, and in addition to being pretty, she was funny, outgoing, and very athletic. She was the only one of the girls who was willing to jump in the lake and give skiing a try—she fell several times, but she kept trying until she was finally able to stand. I was impressed with Becky's tenacity, and before they left I asked if she would call me. I didn't have a pen or paper in the boat, but when we dropped them off at the dock, I told her my number and she repeated it so she could write it down when they got back to their car. My friends and I kept skiing, but my mind was otherwise occupied. I had a feeling this girl was different. I really hoped she would call, and I was kicking myself for not having gone back to my car to take down her number.

After a few days, I still hadn't heard from Becky, and I was starting to worry. I thought I'd been charming as heck that day at the lake, but maybe she just wasn't interested. Should I try to track her down or just let her go? I decided to try to find her. I didn't know where to start, so I just looked up her last name in the phone book and starting calling people, asking for Becky. After a few wrong numbers and a big dose of feeling stupid, I quit dialing random strangers. The next day, she called me. I was surprised, but thrilled, and we set a date for the upcoming weekend. This was March of 1997. I was twenty-four years old, and I had just celebrated four years of sobriety.

When we went out to dinner, I invited another couple along, friends of mine, to help take some of the pressure off, and we ended up having a great time. At dinner, my buddy went on and on about how the story of how Becky and I met was pretty cool, and he even said, "Wouldn't it be funny if you guys ended up getting married?" I kicked him under the table, and quickly changed the subject.

After dinner, I figured Becky and I were ready to fly solo, so we said good night to my friends and went back to my apartment. We just sat and talked for hours. Becky had just graduated from Baylor University with a degree in dietetics and was living with her mother while she did an internship. (Her mother kept calling to make sure she was okay while she was hanging out with me—the guy she met on the freeway.) While we talked that night, I told her all about my new life, and all about my past, because I felt that she was special. I didn't want to screw things up by hiding anything. I figured it was best to put all my cards on the table. I was nervous, though; it was a lot to take in on a first date and I had no idea how she'd react. Fortunately, she was very open to all I'd been through. She actually had a relative who was a recovering alcoholic, so she was sensitive to the struggle.

I knew right away that Becky was exactly the woman I had been looking for, exactly the woman I'd prayed about. She was beautiful, educated, rarely drank, had never done drugs, and certainly didn't seem like the kind of girl who slept around. She lived with integrity and it was evident in everything she said and did. She was, in many ways, the type of person I aspired to be.

Eventually, Becky decided it was getting late and that she needed to be getting home. I walked her to her car and kissed her good night—the kiss was electrifying. Everything in my being was telling me she was the one. Our next date wasn't until about a week later, but we talked on the phone, for hours, every night in between. We had so much in common and shared many of the same beliefs. We both shared a strong belief in Christ, wanted children, liked the same music, and shared many of the same dreams and expectations from life. The list of similarities went on and on. More importantly, we were comfortable with each other and we laughed together constantly. Things between us couldn't have gone any better.

Not everything was rosy, though. I soon met Becky's mother, Sandy, and that did not go so well. Becky had told her all about me and our chance meeting on the freeway, and she apparently thought I was a player. She was very concerned about my background. She didn't trust me, and it showed; she wasn't rude, but she was very standoffish. I just did my best to be polite and hoped that I'd grow on her. When I discussed this situation with my therapist Mark G. (whom I still called for advice), I told him I was just going to sit down with her and tell her what I was all about. He very quickly told me that if I tried to "sell" myself to her, I would end up blowing the whole thing. His advice was to give it time, and eventually she would become one of my biggest supporters. I was skeptical, but he had not steered me wrong yet.

Becky's father, an alcoholic, had died when she was sixteen, but he and Sandy had been divorced since Becky was five. I think the situation with Becky's father was a big factor in Sandy's distrust of me. Sandy raised Becky and her little brother, Nate, on her own, while managing to hold down a job and get a master's degree and a PhD. I appreciate anyone who has that kind of work ethic, but I grew to respect Sandy because of her unwavering integrity and strength. I met Nate a few weeks after that. He was still in school, at Baylor, and although he was very quiet, we seemed to hit if off pretty well.

Becky and I were fairly inseparable from the first date; we genuinely loved doing things together. We were both very outdoorsy and athletic, and we shared a lot of common interests. She was always willing to try new things which I appreciated because it gave me a girlfriend who was also a friend, and allowed me to express my adventurous side. During our quiet times or when the weather was bad, we loved to drive around, cruising through neighborhoods and looking at houses. We would drive for hours, wandering aimlessly through various neighborhoods, just talking and getting to know each other. We both knew that something extraordinary was happening between us. After she finished her internship and found a job, she moved into an apartment near me so that we were able to see each other even more.

Work was still going well, and I was making great money with the partnership I had set up with Ideal Roofing and Siding. They kept me furnished with leads and I was constantly busy. I was still involved in the program, though, and it was extremely fulfilling. I was attending meetings regularly and sponsoring others. My schedule was absolutely perfect. I would wake up around nine in the morning and head out to my client meetings. Then I would come home and relax for an hour before going to the gym around four. After working out, I would spend some time with Becky, in person or on the phone, before heading to a twelve-step meeting at eight. Either before the meeting or after, I would spend some time with friends or guys I was sponsoring. I enjoyed all of the deep relationships I'd developed with the people in the program, and helping other men with their recovery was the most rewarding activity I could imagine. To be part of the recovery process, and to witness the complete transformation of a life, is truly awe-inspiring. It continued to reaffirm my faith that anything was possible.

After Becky and I had dated for about a year, we both felt like marriage would be in the near future. Because of that, or because our relationship was so intense, Becky felt like she needed a little time away to make sure that what we had was real. She said she wanted to take a break from our relationship—for about a month—so that she could make sure what we were feeling was right. She told me this one Saturday afternoon while we were sitting in my car outside of her apartment. It was so unexpected that I didn't know what to say; I immediately started to tear up. I thought everything was perfect between us. All of my fears about being abandoned came rushing back and I felt like I was losing the love of my life. I couldn't hold back the tears and they streamed down my face. I wanted so badly to get angry and lash out, or to bombard Becky with questions about why she was doing this. However, something in my heart told me I had to be loving and supportive. I told her I loved her more than anything in the world and that I would support her in any way she needed. I let her know that I would wait for her as long as I had to and that I was not going anywhere. I reaffirmed that she was the woman for me and that I believed that God put us together for a reason.

After she got out of the car and went into her apartment, I sat in my car and sobbed until I calmed down enough to pray and ask God for guidance and patience. I hoped and prayed that Becky would actually come back to me after the month was up. Then I called my sponsor Scott B. to talk through what was happening. His advice was to leave it up to God, go to a meeting, and spend some time helping someone else. This was his advice on most every issue, and it always worked.

During our month apart, I kept myself really busy with work. A large hailstorm had hit an area about an hour outside of Houston, so I was out of town six days a week, working on that. The timing of the storm was good for me, as it kept me from thinking too much about Becky. In my mind, I knew the break was a good idea; I wanted Becky to be 100 percent sure before we made any commitments. But in my heart, I was miserable and anxious. We had agreed that we were free to see other people during this time, and I went on a few dates, but it was a halfhearted attempt. It just wasn't what I wanted at all—Becky was what I wanted. Everything in my heart told me she was the one. There was just no way that meeting her on the freeway, right after I prayed about finding someone like her, was a coincidence.

On the last day of our month-long separation, I called Becky. My palms were sweaty. But when she answered, she said, "I was just about to call you," and I knew it was going to be okay. We decided to spend a weekend together in Galveston, and it was wonderful. I went all out, getting us a really nice suite in one of the nicest hotels in Galveston, and we had a blast that whole weekend. We went out to wonderful dinners, rollerbladed along the seawall, and went for walks on the beach. It was really romantic. I was trying to re-impress her because it felt like the way we should restart everything now that we were back together again.

That weekend, she told me that she was ready to move forward in the relationship. The time apart had really given us both a chance to realize that this wasn't puppy love; what we had was special, and we were meant to be together. During one of our talks, I asked her what had caused her to come back to me. She said that when she saw how I reacted when she told me she wanted to take a break, she knew I was the one. Part of what she wanted to do was see how serious I was about the relationship. She also wanted to know that I was serious enough to sacrifice a month to support her wishes. We left Galveston after the weekend ended and I was walking on clouds. The girl I loved had come back to me and at that moment in time, life couldn't have been better.

Financially, I was moving up in the world. Because I was tired of living in an apartment, I decided it was time to buy a house. One afternoon, my realtor called to tell me that she had found a great older home in a good neighborhood. It was a fixer-upper, but I worked in construction, and she knew I could turn it into something nice. My realtor and I drove out to take a look at it that same afternoon. As we got close, she began reiterating that whole "fixer-upper" thing, and I started to feel a little apprehensive. Exactly how much fixing up were we talking here? Nothing prepared me for the first look at that house. It was a 1950s ranch house that was painted pink. At first, I thought that might be all the realtor had been nervous about. When we got inside, though, I saw that it got worse. It was also pink on the inside—pink walls, pink carpet, and, you guessed it, pink tile in the bathroom. It was like a full-size Barbie Dream House. It was absolutely repulsive (at least to me). However, I knew I could change that because the house did have some redeeming qualities—a good layout, nice-sized rooms, and an excellent location. It also had great hardwood floors under the awful pink carpet. After walking around a bit, I decided to move forward with the deal.

Within a few short days, the seller accepted my offer and I was on the road to purchasing my first home. Unfortunately, Becky didn't get a chance to see it before I placed my offer. I had made a quick decision because I knew the house would go fast if I didn't sign a contract. After my offer was accepted, I showed Becky the house. She wasn't impressed. When we pulled in the driveway, she looked at me for a moment and then said, "You bought this?" I told her all about my remodeling ideas, and despite her skepticism, she decided to trust me on this one. I closed on the house thirty days later, moved in, and began the remodeling. I did a lot of the work myself, like installing tile, hanging crown molding, and replacing the sink and lighting fixtures. Becky and our friends helped, and we all had a lot of fun in the process.

Shortly thereafter, another large storm hit in Minnesota, and there was a major opportunity to make money repairing the damaged homes and businesses. The remodel wasn't quite done, but it was close, and Becky and my friend Chris K. said they could finish the work while I was out of town. (Chris K., aka Mr. Pasty, was going to be my roommate in the new house. I'll always be grateful for his lack of a tan.) I left for Minnesota with the intention of returning to Houston when the first snow started up there. I also planned to come home every few weeks to see Becky. She was still living in her apartment and working at a dietetic consulting firm, so she needed to stay in Houston. After I got things established in Minnesota, Becky came to visit and we went to a jewelry store to look at engagement rings. We hadn't officially gotten engaged yet, but we both knew it was coming.

We had been dating for almost a year and a half, and my plan was to propose at the eighteen-month mark and then get married six months later. I had been consulting with Mark G. on a regular basis to try and follow his suggestions about how to do things right in this relationship. He thought eighteen months was plenty of time to date before getting engaged, and that six months was plenty of time to wait before getting married; anything longer than that would mean we were stalling or wasting time.

Before I left Minnesota, I bought the ring Becky had liked most and made my plans for proposing. The ring had a round one-carat diamond set in between two round quarter-carat diamonds. The band was platinum and had soft, rounded edges. I must have looked at that ring a thousand times between the time I left the store and the time I actually proposed. I was so excited about the thought of putting it on Becky's finger. I had never felt so sure about anything in my entire life. In Minnesota, I devised a perfect, elaborate proposal. When I returned home, though, the ring was burning a hole in my pocket and I simply couldn't wait. I casually asked Becky to dinner at a nice, five-star restaurant on a Wednesday night. She knew something was up—we didn't go out to five-star restaurants on Wednesday nights. I thought I was being sly by asking her casually, but I found out later that she knew what was coming all along. I never have been able to fool her. She had also seen me out in my car, which is where I kept the ring. I didn't want to have it around the house where she might find it, so I had been keeping it in the center console. She had seen me and my buddies go out to my car and look at something, and she knew what was up.

At the restaurant, I asked for a private table, and we were seated in a quiet, dimly lit corner of the room. During dinner, I got down on one knee and told her how wonderful she was and how I felt like God had put her in my life. I told her I believed that our meeting on the freeway that day wasn't chance, but that I believed God wanted us to be together. I told her that she made me a better man because she showed me what true love, compassion, patience, and kindness looked like; I wanted to be a better person to be worthy of her admiration and respect. Then I asked her if she would spend the rest of her life with me. She said yes, and we both cried tears of joy. Our love was so intense, and yet so natural, that we knew we were meant to be together.

After dinner, we went for a long drive and talked about our relationship and what we wanted in the future. We daydreamed about our life together and all the things we wanted to do. We imagined what our family would be like. We also talked about breaking the cycle of divorce in our family, which was something we both really wanted. We both cried as we drove around, overjoyed and dreaming about our future together.

We told everyone about our engagement right away. All of my friends and family knew what I had been planning, so I shared the good news that Becky had accepted my proposal. I think some of them were actually surprised I was lucky enough to land an amazing woman like her. Everyone was happy for us—even Becky's mom. She and I had really grown close and she had finally let me into her heart. Mark G. was right about her becoming one of my biggest supporters.

When we talked about the proposal and the upcoming wedding, we had a good laugh about a conversation that Sandy and I had had early in the relationship. Becky, Sandy, and I were driving to eat lunch one afternoon when Sandy and I started a discussion, while Becky was in the backseat. We were talking about the future, and I said, "Becky and I will live together after we get married."

"I shouldn't be so sure about having Becky as a wife," Sandy replied.

"I will have her."

"I'll see about that."

"Hello?! I'm sitting right here!" Becky said, breaking up our banter. "I'll be the one to decide who will have me!"

Shortly after our engagement, one of my close sober friends, Matt, who lived in Austin, decided to start a software development company. I had met Matt a couple years before in an odd way: we had both responded to a radio ad for drug study participants. They were offering five hundred dollars for participating in a study for an antipsychotic. The study required that you arrive on Friday afternoon at five and stay in a dorm for the weekend. They administered a small dose of the drug and then drew your blood every six hours. I was accepted into the study, and when I arrived I saw Matt sitting on a couch, typing away on his laptop. This was the mid '90s, and back then people did not take laptops everywhere they went; my first thought was that this guy was a total nerd. I found out later that when I had come in talking on my cell phone, Matt's first thought was that I was loud and obnoxious. We both judged the book by the cover, but by the end of the weekend we had become good friends and we've been friends ever since. I learned a good lesson that day about the importance of looking deeper before judging someone, and keeping an open mind.

About two years after we met, Matt asked me if I would come on board with him as a partner in his software company, as head of business development. I was incredibly flattered. I didn't have experience with the Internet or software, but Matt said he knew that what I lacked in knowledge, I would make up for in hard work. I had already realized that doing insurance work, with the traveling it involved, was not a good long-term plan for me, since it would be hard on a marriage and family. So, I accepted his offer and we got started building an Internet software company. I spent hours and hours immersing myself in reading and asking questions to learn everything I could about Internet technologies. I didn't want to let Matt down, and this was a huge opportunity for me to get into a new field. This was during the Internet boom, and the business grew very quickly.

In the meantime, Becky and I were planning our wedding, and the house had turned out great. (It was now a nice, normal off-white.) Becky was looking forward to moving in and decorating. We began looking for a church that we could not only get married in, but that we could join and start attending regularly. We sought to integrate regular worship and church fellowship into our relationship, as well as into the family that we would eventually have. Becky had grown up going to church, so she had a good foundation. As you know, I found my spirituality as an adult, in the program. I had attended a few churches on and off, but I'd never really found one that felt like a good fit. I believed in God, and I now had a pretty strong relationship with Him, but I continued to be uncomfortable with organized religion.

I had recently been debating Christianity with my roommate Chris K., who was opposed to it. He was very hung up on whether or not the events in the Bible were historically and factually true. I argued that whether or not every word written in the Bible was historically factual was not the point. The principles and the message were what were important. They were what gave me fulfillment, inspiration, and strength. I reasoned that if my beliefs turned out not to be true, then at the very least I would have lived my life believing in something good, something that brought me purpose and joy, and something that made me a better person. I could not think of anything more depressing than going through life believing that nothing matters and that life has no great purpose—that was the life I had lived for twenty years. I also told him that I believed that whatever form of God someone chooses could be good, and that I supported each person's right to his or her beliefs. However, I explained to Chris K. that the only God I know is Christ, and that I could only share my truth and my experience with him and others.

The fact of the matter is that the miraculous transformation in my life was the result of my relationship with Christ. Becky and I shared this belief, and we visited numerous denominations in our search for a church home. We came across a few churches marked by hypocrisy, intolerance, and fire-and-brimstone mentality. But one day, a friend told us about a Methodist church where love and acceptance were both preached and practiced. We visited it, fell in love with it, and decided to join right away. During our very first sermon, both Becky and I were on the verge of tears. I knew right away that I had finally found the church for me, and thankfully Becky felt the same way. It is an amazing place and it soon became an important part of our lives.

On May 22, 1999, we were married at Chapelwood United Methodist Church, by our own pastor, Jim. It was one of the best days we've ever known. Our families came from all around the country and it was a wonderful experience that brought us closer to each other and our families and friends. Our careful planning panned out and the ceremony was absolutely amazing and beautiful. Jim had us write our own vows in addition to the marriage vows he had prepared. I cried my way through my vows; there wasn't a dry eye in the church. My dad was my best man and I was pleased with his participation. We both had changed a lot over the past few years and our relationship was stronger than it had ever been. The highlight was Becky, though. She looked amazing in her white wedding gown. I'll never forget the joy I felt that day. I couldn't stop smiling.

After the ceremony, we had a fantastic reception on the fiftieth floor of a building downtown, and I was literally, and figuratively, on top of the world. We ate and drank (Diet Coke for me) the night away with all of our friends and family. We had over 250 people that cared enough about both of us to share that special day and night with us. Only five years prior to this wondrous event, I had been living in my truck with not one true friend in the world. Now, I had many caring people in my life; I was humbled by the occasion.

The next day, we went to Cozumel, Mexico, for our honeymoon, and had a great time hanging out on the beach and scuba diving together. We had decided to get certified for diving before our trip. It had always been something I wanted to experience, and Becky, being the adventurous person she is, was as excited as I was. We swam with the dolphins, ate wonderful meals, and watched the sunset from our balcony every night. My life was as rich and wonderful as I could have ever imagined. I was married to one of the most extraordinary women I had ever met—the type of woman who would see someone at a party who looked like a lonely outcast and spend the whole night talking to him, making him feel special; the type of woman who lived in a world of black and white, right or wrong, where there were no gray areas used to rationalize bad behavior and actions; the type of woman who always thought of others before herself. I felt more than honored to be her husband. Our honeymoon was as perfect as our wedding, and I was thrilled.

My marriage to Becky also opened a new chapter in my life with my extended family. Over the years, since I'd stopped using, my relationship with my parents had slowly improved. I had worked hard to learn to accept them for who they were, and forgive them for not being who I'd wanted them to be. They had both stopped using drugs and their lives were much more stable. I had also come to realize that, even though they had done many things that caused me pain, they did love and care for me. Slowly but surely, our relationships were mending and growing. My mother and I saw each other fairly regularly, since she lived just outside of Houston, and my dad and I talked on the phone pretty often. Oddly enough, my dad actually started to pursue a relationship with me in a way he never had before. He would call regularly, and he even managed to say "I love you" every now and then. It seemed ironic that once I had reached a point in my life when I no longer needed that from him, he had reached a point where he was able to open up and offer his affection.

Dawn and I had remained close. She had married a guy named Artie, also a recovering alcoholic, who had been sober for quite a few years. He and I hit it off, and as long as he took good care of my sister, I was happy for her. They had four children and life was going well for them. Becky and I decided to have Christmas at our home that year, and everyone was excited to come to Houston. My dad and his wife Gail even planned to fly down for a few days. On Christmas day, the house was all decorated, and Becky had made everything look terrific and welcoming. We had transformed the house from an explosion of pink to the inside of a Pottery Barn catalog and were proud to share our new home with our families.

As we were preparing to eat, I was in the kitchen carving the turkey and caught a reflection of myself in the window. When I saw myself in that window, I remember being struck by how different my life had become. I stood there and reflected on the past and thought about the two totally different lives I had lived. In my addiction, I would have hated the person I was now: khaki slacks, button-up shirt, short hair, sober, working nine to five, and spending time with family. I would have hated that person because I was afraid I could never *be* that person. In that moment, I felt profoundly grateful for all the change in my life, and for the opportunity to become the man I was now. I had grown to love the man looking back at me in the window. I had become a loveable person who lived a respectable life and I had gained self-esteem because I did esteem-building acts. My life was full of people whom I loved and cared for, and who loved and cared for me. The nightmare of my past was no longer destroying my present and I was free to be the person God made me to be. I still struggled with selfishness, ego, pride, and all the things everyone struggles with, but I was no longer ashamed of who and what I was. I was no longer the lost soul that I had been so many years before in that abandoned warehouse. I could hold my head high knowing that I was a good person with a good heart.

Christmas was a wonderful time that year, and I felt my home life and family relationships were on the right track. My professional life was progressing nicely, too. The software business was going well and I had worked diligently to become a self-taught expert in Internet technology. I accomplished this through reading, studying, and talking to as many people as possible about what I needed to learn. I have been gifted with an excellent memory, and the ability to learn and absorb information quickly; I feel very fortunate that my years of drug use didn't take away that God-given gift. Our company had grown from the three of us who started it, to over fifty employees in eighteen months. I was happy with our success and grateful to Matt for giving me the opportunity.

I soon had another reason to feel grateful toward Matt. During our time working together, he suggested I learn to play golf. I was into mountain biking, running, and water-skiing, but I thought golf was too slow a sport to pique my interest. Matt was convinced that more million-dollar deals are done on the golf course than anywhere else, and he said the company would pay for clubs, lessons, and a country club membership. It was an offer I couldn't refuse. I got started with the lessons and practicing shortly thereafter, and I discovered the greatest game ever played. I instantly fell in love. Before long, I sold my ski boat, and my mountain bike began to get very dusty. I found camaraderie, interaction with nature, and a healthy dose of humility on the golf course.

Toward the end of 2000, we received an offer to buy our software company. We all thought we were going to be part of the Internet millionaire boom. After we accepted the offer, the lawyers began work on the purchase contract, which they estimated would take between sixty and ninety days to complete. During that time, the dot-com crash hit. Literally overnight, the company that was going to buy us lost most of their value and then shortly thereafter went under. That meant our deal was over. While we attempted to return to business as usual, it wasn't long before we started feeling the crash as well. Within a few months, we had to shut our doors. We went down twice as fast as we had gone up. The next thing I knew, I was unemployed and looking for a job. Fortunately, my job hunt was successful and I was soon hired by a software company in Dallas to run their Houston office. The skills and knowledge I developed in the technology field over the previous couple years or so allowed me to acquire an upper management position with this new company.

A few months after I began working for them, they informed me that they were closing the Houston office to cut costs. Once again, I found myself out of work. I started looking for a job immediately, but the technology market was in bad shape, and I couldn't find a job anywhere. I was only mildly concerned, though, because I had developed an understanding of faith and was strong in my walk with God. I knew that He would continue to look out for me, just as He had always done in the past. I knew that not everything would be perfect, and that I might experience pain and suffering, but somehow God would find a way to create a good opportunity from a bad situation.

Around this time, there was a huge flood in Houston, and I knew this would be a great chance to do insurance repairs on all the flood-damaged homes. Colin H., who was my first roommate out of treatment and still my best friend, was also unemployed due to the technology crash, and he and I decided to start a construction company. We quickly set up our company and began marketing ourselves in areas that had been damaged by the flood. Since there were more damaged homes and businesses than there were available contractors, we immediately had as much work as we could handle and the business took off. We were working seven days a week, for twelve to fifteen hours a day. I was enjoying the success of the business, but the hours and stress were incredible. Still, the stress of work would soon be nothing compared to the stress of a struggling months-old marriage.

CHAPTER 7

Becky and I had been living together for a little while, and our relationship had started to take a turn for the worse. There were no major blowups, no "one thing" that threatened our marriage; we just weren't feeling or acting the way we had before. Neither of us really understood the problem, but we both felt it, and it was scary. We were growing apart and we had only been married a short time. The bliss of dating was over, and the realities of spending a lifetime with another person set in. We didn't laugh as much, we began doing more things with our friends than we did together, and, for some reason, the fire in our love was flickering. Part of me wondered if we would be able to make it; Becky voiced the same concerns. I was afraid of losing Becky and my marriage, and I really had to tap into my faith and the tools that I had learned in my journey thus far to work through this difficult time.

One Tuesday evening I went out and had dinner with some of my sober friends, including a couple of older guys that

I really looked up to. These men had all been sober longer than I had, and they had successful lives and marriages. I shared with them what was going on at home and they suggested a couples therapy program they had completed a year earlier that had truly changed their lives and their marriages for the better. I immediately spoke to Becky about it. At first, she was against the idea. Becky didn't feel as if she had any emotional issues that were affecting her, or our relationship. Since I had plenty of experience with therapy and seeking outside help, it was natural for me to seek guidance in situations that were not working the way I felt they should. Like many people, Becky felt that she should be able to handle everything by herself, and she did not understand that unresolved emotional issues and a lack of relational tools were the reasons we were struggling. After I explained to her that I really felt her father's death and the circumstances of her parents' divorce had an ongoing effect on her, she decided to give therapy a try. I also explained to her that neither of us had parents that modeled healthy marriages for us—we were both products of divorced families. This could be our opportunity to get the tools we needed to break the cycle of divorce and marital dysfunction. She agreed to give it a try and I made an appointment the next day for us to go check out the therapy program.

We went to a preview of the program before deciding to enlist. We liked what we saw and heard, so we signed up for the four-month program. Every Monday night for three hours, and one weekend a month for eight hours on Saturday and eight hours on Sunday, we attended the couples therapy session. This was a big time commitment, but we knew our marriage was worth more than a few extra hours away from our normal pastimes. It was done in a group format with eight other couples and the counseling was designed to be part educational and part therapeutic. At first, the idea of working within a group was a little scary, but we very quickly grew close to nearly every other couple in the room. We learned from the struggles they were going through, and it was good to know we weren't alone in our marital problems.

In four months, we covered every facet of relationships and marriage. I had once said jokingly in the past that nobody had ever given me the manual on relationships; well, they did in this group, literally—it was four inches thick. Overall, the program was amazing and beneficial. It provided Becky and I with the tools necessary to build a healthy, successful marriage.

Our first lesson in therapy was on proper communication. We learned that whenever one of us was upset with the other, we needed to discuss the situation with "I statements," not "you statements," which sound like accusations. So, for example, I say, "When you do this, Becky, I feel this way." That way, she hears the action or what happened, and then I explain how I feel about it. In addition, we learned to avoid words like *always* and *never*, because they really don't apply. Nobody *always* does anything or *never* does something. Another tool that was helpful was called "negotiating for change." Using the above example, if I began by saying, "When you do this, I feel this way," I'd follow it with "Would you be willing to do it this way or make this change?" Then, I would make an agreement with Becky. It's like a negotiation, rather than a confrontation with only one winner.

Verbal communication wasn't the only form of communication that we learned about. Another important tool we developed in couples therapy was "contracts for the future." In this exercise, one person sits down and draws up an agreement, in writing, about what he or she wants for the future of the relationship and how he or she wants things to happen with the household, kids, religion, money, and all of the other critical pieces in a relationship. The couple reviews the contract, negotiates changes, and decides, as one, how their relationship is going to go. Then they sign the contract as an affirmation of their commitment.

In addition to learning communication techniques, over the course of that four-month program, we had to go back into our childhoods and look at what kind of paradigms we brought to our relationship. What were the belief systems or behaviors we grew up with that conditioned us? It's amazing how many little things are done differently from family to family—and it's really amazing how crazy it can make you when your spouse doesn't do them the way you're used to. A perfect example of this is phone etiquette. Growing up, I would pick up the phone and say hello, the person on the other end would say, "Is Dawn there?" and I'd put the phone down and scream Dawn's name at the top of my lungs until she answered the phone. In Becky's household, things were done a bit differently. She'd pick up the phone and say hello, and the caller would say, "Is Nate there?" and she'd respond, "Yes, just one moment," and then she'd walk all over the house until she'd located him. So when I was screaming through the house for Becky to pick up the phone, it drove her crazy because she thought I was being rude. Neither way is inherently wrong or right; it's just how we grew up. But it's a small example of the kind of things we learn as kids, the conditioning we undergo—"This is how Mom and Dad did it." The program taught us to examine the kinds of habits and idiosyncrasies we brought to our relationship and what effects they had on our daily lives.

In addition to the counseling, we participated in trust-building exercises and individual therapeutic work. The individual therapy helped us deal with unresolved issues from our pasts that were causing us to have difficulties in our relationship. Getting married had caused buried issues related to our parents' marriages to come to the surface for both of us. Becky figured out that she did have emotional issues related to her father's death that were affecting our relationship, and I had issues related to my mother that were also affecting our relationship. Once we got married, we started to transfer some of the energy from those unresolved situations onto each other. By dealing with those issues, we were able to start enjoying each other again.

As we were nearing the end of our four months, I had the feeling that Becky and I had acquired the tools and done the work we needed to do in order to survive and thrive for a lifetime. Of course, just like anything else in life, if we failed to apply what we'd learned, we could end up right back where we started. It was such a relief to regain the confidence that our marriage could last a lifetime—that was the confidence I had married Becky with, but had lost. Now my confidence and faith in our ability to make it was stronger than ever.

Both Becky and I came from divorced families. We never had parents who were able to model for us the way to have a successful marriage and, unfortunately, people aren't born knowing how to be good spouses. We found what we were looking for in this program, and we continued to participate in its ongoing group sessions for nearly a year after the initial four-month program. With every major life change I go through, it seems that old scars resurface, and I have to deal with them. Each time it's painful to confront them, but when I come out on the other side, I'm better, stronger, and healthier. In the old days, I used drugs and alcohol to deal with pain and fear; now I was facing my problems head-on, with the help of God and others.

Due to my hectic work schedule and the marriage counseling, my involvement in the twelve-step program had begun to slip. Work had become all-consuming, and what time I had left over, I dedicated mainly to my relationship with Becky. I attended meetings sporadically, when it occurred to me or when I had a free night, but this didn't happen often. I rarely, if ever, felt the urge to drink or use drugs, so I didn't feel that this lapse in attendance was dangerous. Life had gotten so good and so full that I decided I could ease up on working the program.

Becky had been working at a cancer hospital for about a year, advising patients in palliative care. These were patients who were nearing the end of their lives, and while helping them was rewarding, it was also emotionally draining and took a huge toll on her. She was ready to get out of the hospital environment and had always wanted to start her own business. She had watched me build my business, and the thought of being her own boss excited her. One afternoon, Becky came home and announced that she wanted to quit her job and start her own business. My partner and I were still doing very well in the construction business, so we were in a good place financially and it seemed only fair that she have a shot at doing what she wanted to do. I told her that I would support her in any way possible, and we began discussing various businesses that interested her.

She liked the idea of opening a restaurant, a coffee shop, or a landscaping company. We decided that the restaurant was too expensive to start, and the hours were not conducive to family life. Plus, restaurants were very risky, especially in Houston where the competition was fierce. The coffee shop would probably not generate a large income, so we settled on the idea of a landscaping company. Becky had been taking adult education classes in gardening and landscaping from a retired landscape architect named Dwight, who had sold his own successful landscaping company in the late eighties. He had taken a liking to Becky, as most people do, and he told her that if she wanted to start a company, he'd help out by doing the landscape architecture.

Excited about the prospect of working with Dwight, she told me all about him. She said he was an older guy, maybe around seventy, and he wore hearing aids because he had fought in the Korean War and his hearing had been damaged when a bomb went off in his vicinity. She explained that he was a really cool guy and that I would love him. She said that he struck her as exactly the kind of person I would be at seventy. When I met Dwight, I was as impressed as Becky had promised, by who he was and what he'd accomplished. I learned that he was the oldest living landscape architect in Texas and world-renowned. He had been the American Society of Landscape Architects' man of the year and had developed entire cities. He developed the whole city of Clear Lake—everything from the golf courses to the streets and neighborhoods. He won countless awards in his forty years in landscape architecture, and has just about seen it all. For us to be involved with somebody like that, who could bring clout to the company, was a big deal.

My business partner, Colin H., agreed with my assessment of the profitability of the landscaping venture, so we decided to provide the start-up money and use the construction company's office and clerical staff to handle the work of the new business. We knew we could market the landscaping company to our network of construction clients. The three of us decided that Colin H. and I would be the majority owners and Becky would be a minority owner. We put this plan together in December of 2001, and decided to launch the company to the public in February of 2002. This plan gave us plenty of time to get everything set up and be open in time for the busy spring season. Our intention was to build a solid organization and then sell the company within five years. I had come so close to selling the software company before it fell through, and I still dreamed of successfully building and selling a business.

We got a couple of great breaks right away. In addition to Dwight's help with landscape architecture, one of my acquaintances was a local radio personality who had a gardening talk show. We asked if he'd be willing to become a paid endorser and advertiser for our company. We were thrilled when he agreed, as we knew this would give the company instant credibility and an influx of leads.

Colin H. did not take an active role in the new company because he wanted to stay focused on construction; Becky and I were doing all of the work. She handled the actual project management, I handled sales and marketing, and together we handled the operations aspect. As I had always done before when beginning a new enterprise, I studied and learned everything I could about landscaping in order to become an expert as quickly as possible. I immersed myself in reading, and I took some adult education classes from Dwight to gain more detailed knowledge.

At the same time we were starting the company, I found a flooded house and lot for sale. It was priced way below market value and I saw a great opportunity to buy the lot and build a house. The lot was really big, with a ravine in the back and a several large trees. Becky and I scoured the Internet to figure out what kind of house we wanted to build; we looked at and considered every kind. Right away we were drawn to a Craftsman-style home. It would fit well in the older neighborhood, which was in a historic section of Houston and had a lot of ranch- and cottage-style houses. We chose a plan for a house that was two stories and very homey. The design included a big front porch, which I decided I would immediately hang a porch swing on. It was to be a really nice, cozy, cottage-y house.

Our first house had substantially increased in value, and when it sold, our profit paid for a substantial portion of the new lot. I acted as the general contractor for our new home and Becky helped with the non-construction-related tasks, like choosing finishes, scheduling deliveries, and picking things up if need be. Between the two of us, we must have made a hundred trips to hardware stores and construction supply companies. This was a bold move—building a house at the same time we were starting up a company—but I knew this lot was a great deal, and I knew we could flip the house in a couple years and make great money. We moved into a small apartment while we built the new house, which was scheduled for completion in six or seven months.

This was an incredibly difficult time for Becky and me personally, because there was so much going on in our lives. I was really struggling with being responsible for the direction and management of both companies. I was in charge of handling the financial and operational aspects of the businesses, as well as selling jobs when I was able. I really felt that the success of both companies rested squarely on my shoulders. Neither Becky nor Colin H. had any experience starting and running a business, so they both relied upon me to be the guiding force.

Colin H. had been steadily slacking off more and more, to the point where I would have to call him to find out if and when he was coming to work. Our relationship was deteriorating rapidly, due to his lack of dedication and effort. Becky and I worked from six in the morning until nine at night, six or seven days a week, while Colin H. kept bankers' hours. This lopsided arrangement created some real animosity in me.

Despite this, our landscape company was up and running. We sold our very first job, which would turn out to be the most hilarious project we ever did. We didn't really know anything about landscaping at that point—that is, we'd taken Dwight's classes and read books, but we'd never actually built a job. So, Becky and I solicited the guy who mowed our yard to come into business with us, along with his laborers. They had no experience with landscaping; they only mowed lawns for a living. In short, our learning curve for this first job was as steep as the walls of the Grand Canyon.

Dwight had drawn an architectural plan and had shown us how to do the measurements, the lines, and everything involved in the layout, but we hadn't yet done the actual work. We did okay following the plans, with one major exception— we misunderstood how many bags of fertilizer we were supposed to use per square foot. Instead of using what I later found out was standard for a yard this size, about four bags, we used *forty*. (Luckily, we were into organic fertilizer which won't hurt anything; it'll only help it.) So we put forty bags of fertilizer down in these customers' yard, and it took us *forever* to do it. We put all the plants in, and it was a beautiful job. The clients were happy and despite massively overspending on fertilizer, we actually made a little profit. The funny part was that the customers' yard turned into a jungle overnight, and all their neighbors asked how we did it. (We didn't tell them.) They all wanted us to work a miracle on their yards as well. The job took longer and cost more because none of us knew what we were doing, but in the end, everything was perfect, the clients were happy, and we got a whole slew of referrals.

Everything was moving full speed ahead. Becky was waking up at five o'clock every morning to get the workers and materials lined up for each day's work. At that point, we had five employees and one truck, with Becky managing the jobs. She was out in the hundred-degree heat, working with the crews and managing the jobs all day, which would take a toll on anybody. We were both working twelve to fifteen hours a day, seven days a week, and then working on the house when we could find any spare bit of time. I had begun to develop stomach ulcers, because the stress was so intense, and I was eating antacids like they were candy. My prayer and meditation time had also fallen by the wayside; by the time I finally fell into bed each night, I was asleep within seconds.

About six months after we started the landscape company, the problems with Colin H. finally reached a point where I couldn't continue to work with him anymore, but I didn't want to jeopardize our friendship by confronting him. I discussed the situation with Becky and decided I was going to meet with Colin H. The plan was to explain that I no longer wanted to be involved in the construction business and that I wanted to work with the landscaping company full-time. I had developed a genuine passion for landscaping, and that business was taking off. I would offer to split both companies—he would own 100 percent of the construction company, and Becky and I would own 100 percent of the landscape company. I also planned to tell him that we would be moving to another office location.

In the process of discussing this proposal with him, I wasn't completely honest about why I was making this big change. We had been friends for a long time and I didn't want to have to tell him that he was the reason I wanted to leave. His lateness, laziness, and all-around lack of dedication to both companies made for an unpleasant and stressful working environment. It wasn't fair for Becky and me to have to carry the burden alone. In hindsight, it would have been better to have been upfront with him, because he was angry about my decision and developed a resentment toward me for leaving. If, upon entering the discussion with him, I had told him how his actions were the catalyst for my departure, it might have stung, but maybe he'd have placed some of the blame where it belonged, and maybe he'd have learned from it. In the end, we agreed to split the companies, but it cost me a friend. It was a high price to pay, for both of us.

Now that we no longer had the income from the construction company, and since the landscape company wasn't breaking even yet, Becky and I had to live off of our savings. This was obviously a very scary time for us. We were burning through our savings fast and had no idea whether the landscape business was going to make it. I borrowed a little bit of money from a friend to help us stay afloat and subsidize our advertising. In return, he was given a percentage of the company, in addition to the future repayment of the debt.

It took a long time for the business to start making money. Every dollar that we brought in was swallowed up by our overhead and payroll. In addition, we had a lot of start-up costs. There were many times in those first twelve to eighteen months when Becky and I really questioned ourselves. "Should we quit? Are we going to make it? Is this the right thing?" When you're working seventy, eighty hours a week and not seeing any profit, just getting more debt, you naturally begin wondering if you're doing the right thing. More than once, we came close to giving up, but in the end we managed to work through the fear. When things get tough and scary, and Becky and I find that we are in a jam, we don't freeze up, but instead go into manic hyperactivity. We work faster, we work longer, we try harder. Our work ethic, along with God's grace, is what got us through the incredible stress we were experiencing.

Adding to our financial strain, Becky and I were also putting a lot of money into the new house. With both of us working incredible hours and worrying about money, this time really tested our faith and our marriage. We had to operate as a team 100 percent of the time in order to make it through this period. For the sake of our marriage, we began going back to our couples therapy to help get support for our relationship and to strengthen our bond.

Our first office for the new company was a tiny warehouse, about the size of a walk-in closet, with no heat and only a little window air conditioner that barely kept the room below ninety in the summer. In the winter, Becky would work at the computer bundled up in a jacket and gloves. Our desks were crammed into the room and anytime we were both on the phone, we had to try to hold a conversation with a client without it sounding like we were sitting in the middle of a telemarketing center. We used to laugh when we would come back to the office and find rats on our desks, eating our snacks. Needless to say, it was a very humble beginning.

We both wanted to build the kind of company that would represent all of the good attributes we had seen and experienced in other companies, while avoiding the pitfalls and bad habits that can ruin a company's reputation. We made a conscious effort to put our clients, employees, and suppliers ahead of ourselves. We made sure we consistently acted with honesty and integrity in all of our business dealings. We refused to cut any corners, regardless of the cost. We had both seen the damage done when a company cuts corners and cheats people. With my old partner, Charlie D., I had personally experienced how greed on the part of the owner can cause the whole thing to crumble. We knew that if we took care of our employees and our clients, they would take care of us.

There was also a real opportunity in the landscaping industry for a company to come into the market and dominate by operating at a higher level. Most companies in the green industry are run like mom-and-pop shops; even though we were small and young, we operated and acted as if we were a national outfit. By bringing this big-picture attitude to our company and practicing these principles, we grew very quickly and profitably. After about fifteen months of hard work, Becky and I finally began taking paychecks. We soon moved from the warehouse with the rats, which was rented, to another warehouse and office area, which was the first building and property we purchased. As we continued to expand, we needed a bigger facility, so we bought the adjoining land—it was almost an acre with a huge warehouse and offices. Now we owned almost the whole block. This was a long way from sharing lunch with the rats, and Becky no longer had to wear her ski gear to do office work in the winter.

My plan for the company was to provide more services than just landscaping to our clients in order to expand our market share. The services I felt would work well with landscaping included landscape architecture, pool construction, and commercial facility maintenance. We also focused on winning the larger and more difficult projects where there was less competition and the fees were higher because of their complexity. The business itself became very complex in order to attain proficiency in so many areas. The hard part in managing all of this was finding good people who were experts in their respective areas, and then taking good care of those employees so that they'd remain loyal. I developed this strategy when the company was still in the planning stages, and now it was working out very well. After about eighteen months, we had enough staff to allow Becky to fully concentrate on the accounting and process side of the business, allowing our project managers to handle their projects. I spent most of my time working on sales and marketing activities, as well as supervising our project managers. I also focused on implementing the vision and direction for the company in order to reach our growth, revenue, and profitability goals.

Our growth was exponential and the challenges we faced were mounting, so someone from our couples therapy group suggested that we hire a business coach to help us. At first, I had the attitude that I knew what I was doing and didn't need to pay for advice. When I shared these thoughts with a friend of mine, he pointed out that even Tiger Woods, the best golfer in the world, had a coach—what made me think I wouldn't benefit from a little professional insight and guidance? That really hit home for me. I decided to have an open mind about it, and Becky and I met with a business coach named Alistair the following week. He turned out to be very helpful. He provided a third opinion when Becky and I were deadlocked on an issue, and he helped us stay focused on doing the things that are important but tend to get lost in the shuffle—things like planning and analyzing various numbers and trends. He really helped keep us on track, and he took a little of the pressure off as well.

We soon began to get large-scale projects, like huge estate-type properties where we developed and installed complete backyard retreats that cost upward of a half million dollars. We'd design everything, including drains and irrigation, and then go in and execute the projects with our in-house team. We also handled commercial projects, like high-rise apartments and condos. Projects in that area got up to a million dollars, some of which we won national awards for. Dwight was designing all of these projects. He's an amazing landscape architect and incredibly creative, so he was the backbone of the architecture aspect of the company.

After two uphill years with the new business, things were gradually beginning to smooth out. Becky and I were doing well. The work we had been doing in couples therapy had really paid off and I no longer had to wonder how our relationship was going to last, because now we had the tools to deal with the struggles attendant on marriage. I had continued to retain the belief that we would be together for a lifetime, and that we could break the cycle of divorce in our families. We were still working a tremendous number of hours, but the company was profitable, and we were finally settled in our new house. We decided it was time to do something we always wanted to do when we were married but before we started our family: travel. So, we planned a two-week trip to Europe with Becky's mother and her brother, Nate. We flew into London, and traveled around Europe. We spent four days in Scotland, and while we were there, I got to realize every golfer's dream: playing golf at St. Andrews. It was so incredible to play golf there that I felt it was almost a spiritual experience, and I was grateful to get to do it. It was another affirmation of the life I was leading. All in all, it was an amazing trip during a beautiful time of year.

Not everything was going smoothly, though. Becky and I had been trying to get pregnant for eight or nine months without any luck. We were both ready to start a family. Our plan when we married was to have children as soon as we were settled work-wise, and comfortable financially. We also wanted to do a little traveling before starting our family. Now we had accomplished both of those goals; since we started dating, we had been to Mexico, the Cayman Islands, and Europe. We had been working hard and having fun, but now we were focused on starting a family.

Another nine months passed, and still no luck. We had tried so many different techniques for timing, and just about every other suggestion we heard, but nothing was working. We finally decided to go see a fertility doctor who also happened to be a client of ours. She ran a bunch of tests and couldn't find anything that should prevent us from getting pregnant. We then tried artificial insemination to see if that would work. We attempted this twice over a five-month period, and it was unsuccessful as well. Becky was also taking fertility drugs, but the results were the same. It was a very frustrating and emotional time for us. We were both blaming ourselves for not being able to conceive. We felt defective, and we felt like we were letting each other down. I was really feeling fearful that I was the problem—that somehow I had brought this on by all of the damage I must have done to my body with drugs and alcohol. It also caused me to question my manhood and my ability to bring a child into this world.

It was at this time that Nate and his wife of two years, Laura, announced that they were having a baby. This news was really hard on Becky's emotional state. Her little brother was about to have his first son, while she and I, who were exhausting every avenue for success with our typical do-or-die approach, couldn't seem to conceive. To make matters worse, it seemed that everywhere we looked, people we knew were having babies. It felt as if we were missing out on something really special and we wondered if our dream of having children would ever come true.

Our landscaping company now employed over seventy people, and it was a lot to manage. We had established ourselves as one of the top companies in the city and we'd done it in only three and a half years. We had won numerous state and national awards for our work, and the company continued to be highly profitable. Our hard work was really paying off, but we began to wonder if the job stress was affecting our bodies in some way and preventing us from conceiving. We decided that having a family was more important than having a company, and even though we had originally planned on selling at the five-year mark, we decided to put the business up for sale a little early.

We also decided to move forward with a surgical procedure to try and get pregnant. This in vitro surgery was very physically taxing for my wife, and emotionally taxing for both of us. What's more, the procedure didn't work, and the constant failure in conceiving over the last several years was really taking a toll on us. We felt completely helpless, and this wasn't something that we could just work harder to overcome. It was difficult for us to accept and understand why we could not conceive. We were young and healthy, and the doctors couldn't find anything that should prevent us from getting pregnant. We almost wished that they had found something wrong; at least then we'd be able to identify the problem and have something to blame. We felt like we were being punished, but we didn't understand what for. Why was God not allowing us to conceive a child?

My faith was seriously tested by these events. God had always watched out for me and provided for me, and right now this was the most important thing in my life. I so desperately wanted this chance to be a father and to love a child like I had never had a chance to be loved. In some ways, raising a child would be my opportunity to set right some of the wrongs that had occurred in my childhood. This struggle to conceive had been going on for so long, and we had tried so many different procedures without success, that it was beginning to feel hopeless. I kept going back to my past experiences, where, over time, things had always worked out, but that didn't seem to be possible with this situation. It was also hard to be faithful and patient with something so personal and so important to us.

By then, we had met with a few prospective buyers for the business, but we had turned down their offers. We didn't feel that their offers matched what the business was worth. Besides, we didn't want to sell prematurely. During the process of meeting with these prospective buyers, we learned a lot about what would increase the value of the business and what buyers were looking for. We still needed to finish developing the management team, as well as grow our commercial facilities maintenance division, which produced a recurring revenue stream. We went ahead and took the business off the market, hired more staff, and got to work on developing our management team and growing our commercial maintenance division. We also prayed that relieving Becky of some of the accounting stress would help us get pregnant.

In December 2005, we went to a different doctor and tried another surgical procedure to try and get pregnant. This time, they did a pregnancy test a week after the procedure and told us that we were finally pregnant. It was the greatest news we had received in a long time, and it felt like our prayers were being answered at long last. It was just before Christmas, and we couldn't wait to tell our family and friends.

Between the doctors' appointments, the pregnancy, and the business, I had really been letting my involvement in the twelve-step program slide. I had only been going to meetings every couple of months, and I rarely spoke to Scott B. Even worse, I hadn't been very available to the men I'd been mentoring, and most of them had found other men in the program to sponsor them instead. Because I had not experienced that overwhelming pull toward drugs and alcohol for so long, it was all too easy to think that I didn't need the program. But twelve-step programs aren't just about the problems of the past; they're about keeping you spiritually and emotionally fit for the difficulties and challenges that life throws at you. And those challenges will always come. Alcoholism is not a disease that goes away. It's a disease that goes into remission and will only stay in remission if you are taking care of yourself spiritually and emotionally.

My father and his wife came down for the holidays that year, and although our relationship had improved, his actions could still bring back old resentments and insecurities. When I was a child, he used to tell me that I was an accident and he had never wanted kids. He even had what he thought was a funny story about my conception to go along with the assertion. He regularly told this story when I was around and we were in groups of people. I sure didn't find it funny (especially with my present fears of being denied a child of my own) and I doubt anyone else who was present thought it was funny. He was so clueless about his own callousness that he would even talk about his distaste for children in groups of people who had kids, and who apparently enjoyed being parents.

Fed up and frustrated with his behavior, I decided to finally confront him. So that Christmas I wrote a long letter telling him how it felt to hear those things and how painful it was that they were never followed by, "But I sure am glad that Dawn and Derek are my children because they turned out well." I told him that as long as he continued to act that way and say those things, I wasn't going to have a relationship with him anymore. That was a big moment for me, finally stepping up and saying, "No more." It was also another step toward me getting rid of that old message I grew up with that told me I wasn't good enough or worthy. After he read the letter, we talked about what I'd written, and it was a good talk. He never apologized for his behavior, but he agreed to stop talking like that, which was good enough for me.

Over the holidays, we shared the good news of Becky's pregnancy with our families and a couple of good friends, and then waited for our next doctor's appointment, at which Becky would undergo some follow-up tests. The news we received the following week was absolutely devastating. They told us that Becky's body had rejected the pregnancy. Our hopes were shattered. We cried and actually cursed at God on the way home from the doctor's office. That day we not only lost a child, but we also lost the dream of a child. I began to realize we might never be parents. We both felt powerless, and we were angry at God. Why was this happening to us? What did we do to deserve this? It was an incredibly depressing Christmas and New Year's.

But after the holidays were over, we began to feel differently. Nothing had changed since we had received the terrible news, but we eventually came to the realization that even though we couldn't conceive, we could still be parents. We made our amends with God and seriously considered adoption. *There must be a child out there who needs a good home and maybe we were meant to be his or her parents*, we thought. It wasn't an easy conclusion to come to, nor was it a spur-of-the-moment decision, but it was the only thing that seemed to make any sense to us. Neither Becky nor I truly believed God was punishing us or causing us to not get pregnant—though those thoughts came to us in the depths of our overwhelming despair at the death of the child we had such hopes for. We still believed in a loving God and we accepted his will. The bottom line was that for some reason our bodies were not compatible for natural conception.

However, we both believed that God would help us with our desire to be parents in some form or fashion.

I'll admit I was very scared to adopt, because I had no idea what type of child we would get. Would our baby be happy, healthy, and smart? What kind of family would our baby come from? Would it be hard for our baby if he or she didn't look like us? It took a lot of faith just to apply with an adoption agency and wait to see what would happen. We completed the extensive application process with a local agency by the middle of February 2006. A couple weeks later, we were to be visited at home by the agency's social workers to finish the process and become officially eligible to adopt a child. The agency had already explained to us that the adoption process typically takes nine to twelve months. We were okay with waiting—what were a few more months at this point? We had already spent over four years trying to get pregnant. Besides, it would give us the time to get everything ready for the baby. We told the agency that we were open to a child of a different race, and we would be happy with a boy or a girl; we just wanted a healthy baby.

The social workers arrived, and we took them on a quick tour of the house, pointing out the room that would be the nursery. Then we sat in the living room for nearly an hour, drinking coffee and talking. The social workers, two middle-aged women with kind faces, asked us question after question about our lives, habits, parenting beliefs, careers, and personal goals. They sipped their coffee and scribbled down our answers on their clipboards. They also took us each to separate rooms and asked us questions individually about our childhood experiences. In previous paperwork, I had already made the agency aware of my history, and I had also explained the steps I had taken to resolve the issues of my past. I prayed that my child-hood mistakes would not prevent Becky and me from being parents. When it became clear that the visit was drawing to a close, Becky asked them what the next step was. One of the ladies paused, looked at her coworker, looked back at us, and smiled. "The next step is getting that nursery ready," she said. Then she blurted out that a birth mother had already chosen us, and that we had a baby boy coming in thirty days.

CHAPTER 8

It took a few moments for us to process what she had said. Stunned, we both asked her to repeat it. She explained that someone had already chosen us and that we could expect a baby boy in about a month. Words can't possibly do justice to what we felt. Never in a million years did we expect to get a baby so quickly. We both began crying tears of joy as the social worker told us about the birth mother and the planned due date of our baby. She told us that the young mother wanted to meet us at the agency in a few days. She was a college student who had gotten pregnant, but was not in a relationship with the biological father. It was important to her that she finish college, and that the baby have a home with two loving parents who had the means to care for him. The situation sounded perfect.

When we met the birth mother, Katy, we were amazed at how much she looked like both Becky and me; she could easily have passed for one of our siblings. She had long, straight, sandy-brown hair and blue eyes. Her skin was fair, and she was about five feet six inches tall, about the same height as Becky. She had a small build, so at the moment she seemed to be all belly. Becky and I were both very nervous going into the meeting, because we didn't want to do or say anything that might change Katy's mind about choosing us. Until the baby was born and all of the legal paperwork was complete, the baby wouldn't be ours.

We decided to stay focused on sharing with Katy exactly who we are, without trying to tell her what we thought she might want to hear. Our plan was to trust in our belief that God would take care of us, and all we needed to do was focus on doing the right thing. We met with Katy for about an hour and learned about each others' lives. We asked each other questions about family, faith, beliefs, and interests. She was from a very small town up north and had decided to come to Houston to live with her aunt during the pregnancy and delivery. She was a freshman in college and she was enrolled, temporarily, at a local college in Houston to make sure she stayed on track with her schooling. We discussed the delivery and she told us her due date was supposed to be April 16, but she and her doctor felt she would probably deliver a little earlier. Katy told us she would call and let us know when she went into labor so that we could be at the hospital. Before we left, we gave her a hug and told her how grateful we were that she had chosen us to be the adoptive parents.

We felt a strong connection with Katy, and it was an incredibly emotional time for Becky and me. The emotions we felt were a mix of joy for ourselves, sadness for the loss we knew Katy was feeling, and fear that she might change her mind, shattering our dreams again. We had experienced so many failures in our quest to get pregnant that we were afraid we would be let down again. To keep us strong, we prayed and focused on the belief that God had a plan for us and was leading us toward adoption. We were doing what we were guided to do.

The next month was a complete whirlwind of preparation for the new baby and lining up everything at the company so that we could take a few weeks off to spend time with our new son. Becky and I went shopping to stock up on all of the baby stuff we would need, and we went a little overboard. We walked into the store with a huge list of things we thought we might need. Instead of wandering the store in search of each individual item on the list, though, we decided to just go down every aisle, figuring we'd see things we'd forgotten. Boy, did we ever! We looked at every single brand of every single item. "Do we buy this one or that one? This one's more expensive, so it'll probably last longer, but this one's got extra features." Down the first aisle or two, I put the most expensive one of everything in our cart. I figured we shouldn't skimp—only the best for our baby. But by the time we got to the end of the second aisle, I started totaling up our items and realized there was about two thousand dollars' worth of stuff in our basket. And we still had ten aisles to go. We began to backtrack, putting some things back, and started bargain shopping. It still cost us a small fortune.

A few weeks later, we got a phone call from the agency, telling us that the doctor was going to induce labor on March 30, 2006, which was a couple weeks early, and informing us that we should be at the hospital at 8:00 a.m. Becky had been reading baby books to prepare for the big day. I thought I was prepared enough, but the night before our son was to be born, I lay in bed beside her, thinking, and the reality of what was about to happen hit me. I was petrified. I suddenly realized that I had no idea what life would be like with a baby. I rolled onto my side and whispered, "Becky, are you awake?" Of course she was. I asked her, "What do babies do all day?" She laughingly informed me that they sleep for about eighteen to twenty hours a day in the beginning. I was immediately relieved. I could handle that. I only had to figure out what to do with our baby for four to six hours a day. But I was still really nervous about being a good father. I hadn't learned much from my own father, and it was really important to me that I do things differently.

I barely slept, and the next morning I was in a daze of warring emotions, so wound up that I could hardly drive to the hospital. When we got there, the social workers greeted us and introduced us to Katy's grandmother and aunt; they were very sweet, and we bonded with them right away. Katy's grandmother had driven down from Dallas to be with Katy for the delivery. Both of Katy's parents worked full-time, and they were unable to be there. We stayed in the room, talking with Katy and her family, until she went into labor. Then, as we were leaving the room, the grandmother turned to Becky and, removing her wristband, said, "Here, honey. You're the mother. You should be here for this." She handed Becky her wristband so that Becky could remain in the room for the delivery. This generosity brought grateful tears to our eyes; I hugged Becky and then left the room to pray and wait.

Labor went smoothly, and Becky was there to see our son come into the world. After Mattox was born, the doctor began to hand him to Katy, and Katy told him she wanted Becky to hold him first, stating, "She is his mother." I wasn't in the room for this amazing experience, but I know it meant a lot to Becky to be acknowledged in this way by Katy. She was so touched and so elated that she cried her eyes out as she held our son. After holding Mattox for a bit, she handed him to Katy and they both cried and hugged each other as they held him. The moment could not have been more perfect. About fifteen minutes after the delivery, I was allowed back in, and when I held Mattox for the first time, I felt like I was coming apart emotionally. I sobbed tears of joy. I couldn't believe I was actually a father. He was so tiny, wrapped up in the little blanket—five pounds, ten ounces, and twenty inches long. He was cute, with just a little bit of brown hair on the top of his head, and looked like a little turtle with his pointy head and scrunched-up face. I fell instantly in love. Both our families came to the hospital that afternoon and spent time together with Katy, her family, and the star of the show, Mattox Steele.

By law, we could not take Mattox home right away, and Katy could not sign over parental rights until forty-eight hours after his birth. So that evening, we had to drive home without our baby, and hope and pray that Katy wouldn't change her mind. On the one hand, our hearts were breaking for her, and we knew that what she was doing was one of the most difficult and painful things she would ever do. But on the other hand, we wanted Mattox more than anything in the world. We returned to the hospital the next day and spent the day with Katy, Mattox, and various friends and family. It was another wonderful day, followed by another sleepless and terrifying night. The next morning, we went back to the hospital, and this time we brought a car seat so that we could take our son home. I was so nervous and emotional that once again, I had a hard time concentrating on driving and my hands trembled on the wheel.

When we arrived at the hospital, Katy was dressed and out of her bed. Her bags were all packed, and she and her aunt, along with her grandmother, were sitting in the room, holding Mattox and talking. The past couple of days had been light-hearted as we all spent time together, admiring Mattox. Today was completely different, and we could feel the sadness and pain Katy was experiencing. Her eyes were red from crying, and she looked as if she had aged ten years overnight. I felt so much sadness for this wonderful and sweet woman whom we had grown so close to over the past two days.

After we spoke to Katy and her family, and of course looked in on Mattox, the social worker took us to another room to discuss what would take place next. She told us Katy had signed all the papers before we arrived, and she explained that we would say our good-byes to Katy and her family, they would say good-bye to Mattox, and then they would leave the hospital. She told us we would need to sign additional papers, and after that, we could take Mattox home. The social worker then suggested we should all take some pictures together before Katy and her family left. We all went into the hospital hallway to take pictures and say our final good-byes.

The good-bye was unlike anything I had ever experienced. I watched as Katy tenderly touched her son—I imagine that moment must be a lifetime for her now. She cried as she held him, and in her eyes I saw both an aching void and joy. From our earlier talks, I knew she believed she was doing the very best thing she could possibly do in this difficult circumstance.

During this interaction, I could barely speak and words became meaningless and unnecessary. I felt a mixture of sadness, admiration, and gratitude. Faced with the immediate reality of adoption, I was awed that such a young woman would entrust Becky and me with her most prized possession: her newborn son. Katy held Mattox for a time, and then, with great courage, she handed him to us. Tenderly, Becky received Mattox. In my mind, the exchange represented two things—a child for our future and a future for Katy, who herself was still a child.

All the internal work I had done for myself since my decision to beat addiction seemed to lead me to this point. I knew this was what God had in store for me from the beginning of my life—this is why I had endured the things I had and had struggled to overcome them. This was His plan even before He made me see the light in that warehouse so many years ago. With this realization, tears streamed down my face and it was then that Katy looked over at me and silently, with her eyes, let me know she believed she had made the right decision. She was entrusting Mattox to a man with a big heart. As my heart opened with the pain of my epiphany, it also opened up in joy to be blessed with such a gift as this child.

Looking over at Becky and Katy, I saw two mothers—two women who were bonding in both loss and gain. I wondered at how courageous they were; Becky, for entrusting me with her heart and her future, and Katy, for giving her child a better chance at happiness than she felt she could provide. I watched as Katy slowly turned and walked out of the hospital, each step taking her further away from her son. With red swollen eyes she turned for a last look. She saw Becky and me holding Mattox and she smiled, putting her hand over her heart. One last look, and she was gone.

Becky and I cried, deeply hurting for Katy and overwhelmed with joy and love for our son. I was once told in therapy that each feeling is a gift. There is a gift in joy, and there is a gift in loss or pain. They are one and the same—the gift of healing. That day, in that place and moment, two mothers and a dad were healing, becoming stronger as they looked down at the future in their arms—a future filled with love.

After we regained our composure, we finished the paperwork and took Mattox to the car. I was too shaken up to drive, and I just wanted to be close to Mattox, so Becky drove us home while I sat in the backseat with our son. I couldn't take my eyes off of this beautiful little boy. I prayed silently all the way home, asking God to give me the strength to be the father Mattox deserved, and thanking him for bringing this miracle into our lives. I also prayed for Katy and the pain I knew she was feeling. I asked God to give her peace and comfort.

When we got home, all of our friends and family were there waiting for us, and we had a great celebration that afternoon. I was like a mother hen with Mattox; I wouldn't even let anyone hold him until they'd washed their hands. Even then, I hovered over them to make sure he was okay. Everyone made fun of me for being so overly protective, but I didn't care. I had loved him from the moment I first held him, and that love just grew stronger with every minute.

Becky and I spent a few weeks at home after Mattox was born and everything at work went smoothly in our absence. We had built a good management team and our business coach was checking in for us as well. At the moment, our lives were absolutely wonderful. We finally had the child we'd been dreaming of, business was booming, and Becky and I were getting along great. Building the house, starting the business, and struggling with infertility had put a huge strain on our relationship for a long time, but we were finally getting the chance to enjoy each other again, to appreciate all that we had worked for, and to revel in the blessing of our child.

Becky returned to work only part-time so that she could spend more time at home. My mother came down several days a week to watch Mattox while Becky and I were at the office. She was incredible with our son, and I was thrilled to see them bond, but I couldn't help but feel a little sad that she hadn't been able to be present like that with me when I was young. I think, in some ways, she was making up for not being the mother she wanted to have been for Dawn and me. Since she was now retired, she had plenty of time and no distractions in her life. She hadn't remarried after Thomas and had not dated in several years. I think after the experiences she'd had with men, she decided she had had enough of relationships for a while.

I had been steadily drifting away from the twelve-step program for a long time, because I had allowed work and the quest for a child to become the top priorities in my life. And even with the gift of Mattox, I began to feel like something was missing. My relationships with people in the program and the support we gained from each other had at one time given me a lot of fulfillment, and I missed that. Now that we had a new baby, though, I neglected the program even more, because other things had to take priority. I drifted away from many of my sober friends, and I was spending more and more of my free time with businesspeople I had met over the years. They were all good guys, and we spent a lot of time playing golf and poker for entertainment. They all knew I was sober, but all drank, which never bothered me because I enjoyed hanging out with them, playing cards and golf. Besides, it was a good network for my business. Many of the guys I was spending my free time with were very good clients and successful businessmen.

Toward the end of the year, Becky and I decided that we were ready to put the business back on the market. We felt we had developed the parts of the business we needed to develop to make the company attractive to potential buyers. In five years, we had built our company into one of the largest and most respected companies in the city. We had a large and varied clientele, and the business was highly profitable. But we also felt that what goes up must come down, and for nearly five years, our business, and the Houston economy in general, had been booming. These things go in cycles, and it seemed to us only a matter of time before the bottom fell out. We had also concluded that the additional stress that being in business together added to our relationship was not worth it, and that our marriage and our son should be our priority. Working together was wonderful because we were such a great team. However, building, growing, and maintaining the business had taken over our domestic life and we both knew we had more important concerns.

In early 2007, we put the business on the market, and I made sure that we continued to work diligently to keep the growth and profit on the same upward trend. I was working harder than ever because it was critical that we show a consistent growth trend while potential buyers were looking at the company. It was also important to make sure that all of the operational and procedural manuals were up-to-date, and that the accounting and records were perfect. I felt like an athlete in the last minutes of the game—now was the time to make sure everything went exactly according to plan.

Within a couple of months, we received a few inquiries for

the business, and by the summer, we had both a private equity group from the East Coast and an individual buyer preparing offers. We had kept the sale of the business very confidential in order not to disrupt its operations in any way. The offer from the equity group was higher, but they planned on merging our company with several others they were trying to purchase, and the combined companies would be turned into a large company that would service the entire Southwest. The individual was offering us less money, but he planned on keeping the company intact and operating as it always had. This scenario was important to us, because we wanted to ensure that all of our employees would be able to keep their jobs, and that the name and legacy we had built for the company would continue. We had grown so close to our staff over the years that we couldn't bear the thought of them being laid off in the process of mergers and the formation of a conglomerate. After a couple of months of negotiating and deliberating, we accepted the offer from the individual, and the closing date was set for October 31, 2007.

Our plan of building and selling a great business had come to fruition. The company was halfway through its fifth year, and in a very short amount of time it had become a dominant force in the Texas market. It was astonishing to me that we were nearing the achievement of the goal we had set a little over five years ago. We had planned this out, but it still surprised me that it was actually happening. This was a very emotional time for Becky and me, because the company was the product of our blood, sweat, tears, initiative, and time. It had also become a huge part of my identity, and the employees had become like family to us. I knew I would dearly miss all of the staff, as well as the clients. Our plan upon the successful sale of the business was to share a portion of the proceeds from the sale with the employees who had been with us for a long time and whose own sacrifices had greatly contributed to the success of the company. I was really excited to share the news of the sale with everyone and to tell them about the large bonuses they would be getting. I knew this money would make a big impact in their lives.

As the end of October drew near, I began to grow nervous that we were selling too soon and that we should hang on another year or two and potentially sell for even more money. However, I realized greed was seeping in and pushing me to want more money. I resisted the urge to hold out longer, because I realized we could just as easily have a downturn and lose everything. Becky and I discussed it, and in the end, decided to stay focused on the plan and to finish the transaction. Part of the contract of sale would require me to stay on with the company for one year to consult with the new owner and help with the transition. Becky would be able to quit working and be home full time. Having her stay home with Mattox full time was equally important to both of us and we were excited by the prospect.

The month leading up to our closing date had been incredibly hectic. We spent every night and weekend at the office after hours, with the buyer and his legal and accounting teams, carefully combing through records and making copies of everything as a part of the due diligence. Thankfully, we had Becky's mother Sandy to help at the office, while my mother watched Mattox. Without those two helping, it would have been impossible to do what needed to be done. Everything had to be done in secrecy until we announced that the transaction was complete.

On October 31, Becky and I began reviewing the final contract of sale. The lawyers had worked late the night before, making sure all of the documents were correct and complete, and we began the final review together in an office downtown. The contract and all of the supporting documents came to well over a hundred pages and the review process took several hours. A few last-minute changes had to be made before we could all sign, and the lawyers quickly made the changes. Once the contract was complete, the buyer called his bank to process the wire transfer. Even though we had his bank's wire confirmation, our lawyer advised us to wait until we had confirmation from our bank that the wire had been received.

We all decided to go have lunch while we waited. Becky and I had met the new buyer and his wife for lunch a few weeks prior and we felt really comfortable with their personalities and beliefs. We actually had a lot in common with them (they even went to our church, although we had yet to see them there), and we hoped they would maintain the reputation we had worked so hard to build. When we returned from our late lunch, we checked with our bank and were happy to hear that the wire had been received.

The sensation of achieving this huge goal, and then looking at the wire transfer, was surreal. Becky and I were giddy with the realization that we had actually pulled this off. We were multimillionaires, and it had all started with a conversation between Becky and me five and a half years ago. I could now choose to retire if I wanted to, and I was only thirty-five. That wire transfer was a testament to the fact that anyone, regardless of their past mistakes, can turn things around and accomplish any goal they are willing to work for. All the years of working hard, staying sober, and trying to do the right thing had paid off—literally. Becky and I drove home laughing and singing along with one of our favorite songs. We danced in the car (as best as we could), feeling elated and exhausted, like we had just finished climbing Mount Everest.

After the closing of the sale, we introduced the owner to our key staff and made the announcement that we had sold the company. Everyone seemed shocked at the announcement, but they seemed genuinely happy for Becky and me. We assured them that the new owner was committed to keeping the company operating the same as Becky and I had in the past. Shortly thereafter, we called a company-wide meeting to introduce the new owner. He seemed to get along well with everyone, and the transition appeared to be going well.

I soon realized something, though. I had subconsciously been waiting for the money and the accomplishment of the sale to give me fulfillment. I had driven myself so hard, for so many years, not only because I had a desire to succeed, but also because I thought that success would wipe away the last pieces of pain and insecurity that remained from my childhood. Within a few weeks of the sale, though, after the initial excitement had worn off, I realized I didn't feel any different. As a matter of fact, I felt *less* content and peaceful than I had in previous years. Society had programmed me to believe that financial success was the key to true happiness, and yet, when it came, I didn't feel any different. In truth, it was a letdown. With this new emptiness looming, I was afraid that the void in my heart, that had been growing larger for quite a while and had baffled me, was never going to go away.

Becky and I had been discussing adopting another child. We didn't want our children to be too far apart in age, and we knew that it would most likely not happen as quickly with the next baby as it had the first time around. The agency told us that to get a child in forty-five days, as we had with Mattox, was unheard of for an infant adoption. Becky and I felt that now that we had sold our business and Mattox was eighteen months old, we were ready and willing to wait if necessary. Becky was a stay-at-home mom, and my work schedule was fairly light. Plus, in a short while my year of consulting would be complete and I could stop working for as long as I wanted. Being a father to Mattox had been a blast. He was the sweetest little guy a dad could ask for. Nothing could ever compare to holding my child in my arms and rocking him to sleep as he looked into my eyes. I was ready for another child and the timing was good for us. We decided to start the process again and see what was meant for us the second time around.

We went back to the same adoption agency and did all the paperwork necessary to apply for another infant adoption. The adoption coordinator told us that, unlike last time, they weren't currently working with any birth mothers, and that it would most likely be nine to twelve months before we got another child. That was pretty much what we had been expecting, and we were in no real hurry. We were able to complete the application process much quicker this time, and we submitted all of our paperwork in the first week of December 2007. The adoption coordinator asked us if all of our preferences were still the same as before, and we said yes. Basically, we would be happy to have any healthy child. We did tell her that we would love to have a baby girl, but we knew that girls are typically much harder to get, and that we would be happy with whatever child God put in our lives.

The next week, I had plans to go to Vegas with a big group of guys for a golf trip. Before we headed to the airport, we stopped at a restaurant to have lunch. Afterward, on the way to the airport, I received a message from Becky, saying, "We got a baby girl. Turn around." The message didn't register with me. What did she mean, we got a baby girl? We had just filled out the paperwork six days ago. I called Becky right away, and she told me that the birth mother, Tabitha, had contacted the agency while she was at the hospital, and she made an adoption plan with our agency. She had chosen us as the adoptive parents. Our daughter had just been born and we needed to get to the hospital and see her that night. We also had to have a name to put on the birth certificate by that evening. *A name?* We hadn't even begun to consider names! I was shocked speechless. It was so sudden I couldn't wrap my mind around it. One minute, I was heading to the airport for a golf trip, and the next minute I was heading to get Becky to go see our daughter.

I was dizzy with joy and excitement…and a healthy dose of fear. It was all happening so fast my head was spinning. I couldn't believe that I had a baby girl. I had always dreamed of having a little girl—Daddy's little girl. It was another miracle, and this time it took *six days*. The process was a lot different this time. We couldn't take our daughter home from the hospital right away, but we could go see her that night. They needed us to fill out the paperwork and complete her birth certificate. Becky was at the office helping the new owner with some accounting functions when she called me, so I headed to the office right away. When I got there, Becky and I hugged each other and talked about how crazy it was that this was happening. It was unreal that we were going to the hospital in a few hours to see our daughter. We had just a couple of hours to choose her name, so we grabbed a big dry-erase board and started writing names. After an hour of brainstorming and writing names, we had narrowed it down to about five names. We were stuck, so we decided to invite some of the staff that we were friendly with into the office to give us some feedback. Since having a daughter was such a big deal for me, and Becky knew this was important, she let me make the final decision. We chose the name Madison Steele. Madison has always been my favorite name. For me, it conjured an image of a beautiful girl with curly blond hair and big, blue eyes. Little did I know that was exactly what our daughter would look like.

Becky and I drove to the house, where my mother was watching Mattox. We called all of our friends and family to share the good news. Becky's mom left work early, and one of our friends came over to watch Mattox so that Becky and I, along with our mothers, could go to the hospital to see Madison. Becky was on the edge of joyful tears the whole way there, and when we got to the hospital and saw our daughter for the first time, she went over the edge, as did I; tears spilled down both of our faces.

Madison was absolutely beautiful. She had deep blue eyes, a full head of white-blonde hair, and round, chubby cheeks. Unlike Mattox, she had a perfectly round head and a beautiful face. (It took a few weeks for Mattox to get past the funny newborn look.) Both of our mothers were excited, and none of us could stop crying when we held our sweet baby girl.

Tabitha, the birth mother, was a young woman who had a five-year-old son and lived at home with her parents. The biological father lived in another state, and they were not in contact anymore. She knew she couldn't care for another child in the manner she wanted and that adoption would be best for the baby. Tabitha chose not to meet us in person, because, I believe, the pain of her decision was too great. I think she just wanted to try to move on as quickly as possible in order to forget the incredibly difficult choice she had made. After being with Katy and witnessing firsthand the pain and courage it takes to place your child up for adoption, I knew and understood why Madison's birth mother could not bear to see her daughter. I wished that we could have spent time with her like we had with Katy, so that we could have gotten to know her, but I was just ecstatic to have a little girl.

As part of the adoption process, a birth mother looks at books that prospective parents have put together in order to get a feel for what the families are like. Becky and I created our book together, filling it with captioned pictures of our home, our families, our friends, our vacations—every part of our lives was represented in our book. We also wrote a letter to the birth mother, telling her who we are and what our beliefs are. We used the same book for Madison that we had prepared for Mattox's adoption, with the addition of pictures of Mattox and an explanation of how life had changed for us with his adoption.

Going home that night without Madison was one of the hardest things I've ever done. Tabitha had chosen not to stay with Madison at the hospital because she was afraid to hold her and to bond with her. That meant that Madison had to spend the night at the hospital without anyone other than the nurses, and it broke my heart. Becky and I cried for Madison that night as we thought of her all alone at the hospital without us. We knew she would only get a little bit of attention from the nurses, and all we could think of was our little girl all alone without her parents in that hospital all night. We were supposed to pick her up the next afternoon and I couldn't wait to get there and rescue her. For some reason, having to leave her there alone had caused my own feelings of abandonment to resurface. Consciously, I wasn't aware of this, but I knew I felt withdrawn and very sad, and all of these emotions were occurring at a time when I knew I should feel happy and excited.

When we finally brought Madison home, I was numb, because I had been blocking my emotions and trying my best to appear happy. All of our friends and family were there to see the baby, and I was like a robot. My body was working, but my brain wasn't. Becky kept asking me what was wrong and if I was okay. I knew I was worrying her, but I couldn't shake myself out of it. All I could do was not allow myself to feel anything. The fear of raising another child, the lack of time to prepare emotionally for a new baby, and the triggering of my own abandonment issues had combined to turn me into a complete basket case on what should have been a very happy day. Even though I understood on a conscious level why Tabitha had done the things she'd done, it triggered feelings of anger and resentment and depression on a subconscious level. It was more than I could deal with just then.

Feeling overwhelmed by the presence of all our friends and family, I decided I needed to get out of there. Without saying a word to anyone other than Becky, I slipped out the back door and went for a jog. As I ran, I kept thinking about Madison all alone in the hospital, and before long I began crying uncontrollably; as I ran and sobbed, I talked to God. The jog went by in a blur of tears, and most of the time, I was talking to God out loud—if anyone saw me that night, they must have thought I was completely nuts. I asked God to heal my pain and Tabitha's pain, and to protect Madison from any pain she might experience. I also asked God to remove my fears about being a father to these two beautiful children, and to give me the guidance I would need to care for my family. One of the last thoughts and images I had during this run was of Madison, Mattox, and Becky on a beach, and they were all wearing white. As I looked at them laughing and playing on the beach, I envisioned that Mattox and Madison were seven and five years old. They turned and started running toward me, smiling and calling me "Daddy." It was almost as if God had put these images in my mind to assure me that I would be a great father, and we would all be okay.

After this experience, I felt cleansed, and I couldn't wait to get home to my baby girl and hold her in my arms. My heart was open, and I was so excited to begin this new and amazing relationship. When I got to the house and opened the door, I went straight up to my sister and took Madison out of her arms. As I held Madison, I cried tears of joy. At that moment, I let her into my heart all the way. As I looked into her beautiful blue eyes, I fell instantly in love, just the way I had with Mattox. The connection was strong and it felt wonderful to open my heart to this child—my daughter.

A couple days after we brought Madison home, we spoke to our social worker who informed us that Tabitha had come to the agency and signed all the papers. She told us that Tabitha had been devastated by grief and sadness, and had circled around the agency for an hour while she tried to build up the courage to go in and sign the papers to make her decision final.

The social worker said that Tabitha had been crying since she left the hospital, which was a day and a half before, and that she was hurting so bad emotionally, it was showing on her physically. I felt so much sympathy for the loss I knew Tabitha was experiencing. I continued to pray for God to give her peace and comfort in her heart and to help her to know that her daughter would be safe and protected with Becky and me.

Since everything had happened so quickly with Madison, things were pretty hectic around the house. We now had two children in diapers. Madison's swift arrival made shopping for all of her baby stuff easy, though. There was no time to think or debate; we just went to a few stores and bought one of everything pink—my idea of the perfect shopping trip. The fact that Madison and Mattox were so perfect, and had come into our lives so quickly, was nothing short of miraculous, and it once again reaffirmed that God was looking out for us. We had gone through a lot of pain and struggling with infertility to get to this point, but once we opened up our minds and hearts to a different plan—God's plan, not our own—we were blessed with Mattox and Madison. We had no desire to change a thing. Work was going fairly well, except that the new owner didn't want to follow many of the suggestions I gave regarding how to operate the company, which was, after all, the reason I was there. It made it hard to stay motivated and focused at work, but I just reminded myself that it was his company now, and all I could do was offer my guidance and support.

With two young children at home, Becky and I made a big decision. We wanted to move outside the city, into a new house that was larger, and in a neighborhood that was better for the kids. We found a house under construction that had double the square footage of the house we'd been in for the past four years, and we decided to purchase it. It was the type of house we had always dreamed of, and the yard and neighborhood were perfect for kids. Our previous house was very close to downtown, on a fairly busy through street. We had always said we would never move to the burbs, and that we would always be close to downtown, but what was cool and eclectic when we didn't have kids, suddenly seemed dirty and dangerous now that we did. Plus, we wouldn't have to worry about commuting after my transition period with the new owner was complete.

Along with the house, I purchased my dream car—a silver Mercedes S550 with the AMG sport package. It's their top-of-the-line sedan and I'd been fantasizing about it for a while. Driving it was an absolute blast. Every day on the way home from work, I would hop on the tollway, turn on some good music, and just cruise in my new ride. Becky and I were enjoying the fruits of our labor and living our dreams.

That Christmas was a pivotal one in my relationship with my dad. Everyone came down to spend the holiday with us again, including my dad and Gail. We had a really big, happy Christmas. There was a lot to celebrate, most especially a new grandchild. That Christmas, my dad also picked up golf, and he and I played together. Since then, it's become a ritual for us; it's one of the only father-son bonding activities we've ever done on a regular basis. He and I had finally turned a corner where we truly knew and understood each other. Life was good.

After Christmas, as life became routine again, I really began to notice how difficult not owning the company was for me on an emotional level. So much of my identity was wrapped up in being the boss, the owner of a successful company, and a hard worker. For many years, I had put the business first in my life, and it had become more important than it should have been. It had become more important than devoting time to helping others and enhancing my spiritual life; it had even become more important than my recovery and the twelve-step meetings.

The void was still there—inside me. I loved my wife and my children, and spending time with all of them as a family was wonderful, but I needed something more to devote my time and energies to. I felt like I was contributing nothing to society. I tried spending money and surrounding myself with material things, but it didn't work. I just ended up with more stuff and less money, and the emptiness persisted. I was also spending all of my free time with the same guys I had socialized with for business. We spent most of our time golfing and playing poker, but there was not a lot of depth to the relationships—nothing like I had experienced in my relationships with friends in the program. Those relationships were deep and intimate because we understood each other and the struggles we shared. They were also relationships based on mutual support and the search for a deeper understanding of, and relationship with, God. Even though I still had many sober friends, I had drifted away and had not been investing much time in those relationships. With my part-time schedule at work, I was able to attend more twelve-step meetings, but all I was doing was showing up for an hour and then leaving immediately afterward. It was minimal effort on my part to really get connected again. I told myself, *At least I'm going to meetings.* Basically, I was half-heartedly involved.

Around this time, my friend Ziggy and I planned a trip to Mexico. It was just going to be a short weekend jaunt to

Monterrey; we were planning to go see one of my favorite bands, Thievery Corporation. Ziggy was one of my friends who drank; in fact, he owns a couple of bars, and he knew some of the people in the band. He also knew the people putting on the concert. I had missed seeing Thievery when they visited Texas, and this would be one of their last shows of the year. We planned to leave on a Friday morning, and return home late Sunday afternoon.

The Tuesday before we planned to leave, I started to think about drinking and getting high on the weekend trip. I figured I would drink on the plane and drink in Mexico. I also decided I would smoke some pot and do ecstasy if it was available, but I told myself I would stay away from cocaine. I also decided I would come home on Sunday and go straight to a twelve-step meeting to start my sobriety over. When I was contemplating this move, it seemed like a sound plan. I knew Becky would go berserk, but I figured if I went to a meeting when I got home on Sunday, then I could smooth things over and convince her everything would be fine. I was thinking like the addict that I used to be, not like the man I had become.

When I woke up on Wednesday, my mind was made up. I was going to get wasted for the first time in fifteen years, and I figured "what the heck." I had accomplished my goals, I didn't have to worry about work and money anymore, and besides I was bored and felt miserable anyway. I felt empty and unfulfilled, and I wasn't satisfied with myself or with what I was doing with my life. I convinced myself this wouldn't be like before; I somehow thought that I would be able to spend the entire weekend getting wasted on drugs and alcohol, and then come home and start my sobriety over again. It was a crazy and stupid plan, especially considering the fact that I am the type of addict and alcoholic who can't control how much I use or when I stop using. I had never been the kind of person who could stop at one drink or one hit of anything. If I had the ability to start and stop using drugs and alcohol whenever I wanted, then I wouldn't be an alcoholic. I should have known better, known that whatever I did that weekend would start a chain reaction of using. It was an insane decision, because I had nothing to gain and everything to lose.

CHAPTER 9

Looking back, I believe the decision to drink again snuck up on me because I hadn't remained active in the twelve steps and the related service work. I had also allowed myself to become spiritually disconnected. I reached my goals of financial success, and I had surrounded myself with people who were not on a spiritual path. I was spending more time with people who drank than with people who were sober, and none of them focused their time and energy on spiritual growth. I also had not sponsored anyone for a long time, nor had I given my time and energy in service to others. I donated money to some charities, and I tithed to my church every month, but that's not the same as actually doing hands-on work for someone in need. Someone could give money and still be living a selfish and self-centered existence—I was walking proof of that. The feelings of irritability, restlessness, discontentment, and fear had been steadily creeping back into my life. The emotional "unmanageability" had begun to return. I was once again uncomfortable in my own skin.

The Wednesday before the trip to Mexico, I was still planning to move forward with my plan to drink, but for some reason my conscience told me I better call Scott B., my sponsor, who had helped me get sober and stay sober for fifteen years. He and I were very close, and I trusted his judgment implicitly; I knew he could help me sort out all my tangled thoughts. However, I had not spoken to Scott B. in months. I hoped he would be available, but I decided that if I couldn't get ahold of him on the first try, then I would go ahead with my plan. I was testing God again. It was a foolish deal I made with myself, and I knew it, but I made it anyway.

I grabbed the phone and called his office. Scott B. is the assistant dean of a major university and is not usually easy to get ahold of, but he answered his phone after two rings. I proceeded to explain to him that I was planning to drink that weekend, and I gave him all of the details about what I had been feeling and thinking. Scott B. listened patiently, and then told me he was proud of me for being honest, and said that he loved and cared about me. We discussed the fact that working steps ten, eleven, and twelve was a lifelong journey, and that by stopping the work I had invited the insanity back into my life. He suggested that I hit my knees and ask God to remove this insanity and give me the strength to do what I needed to do in order to stay sober. He then suggested that I go to a twelve-step meeting right away and share with the group what was going on with me. His final suggestion was that I go to a halfway house downtown and spend some time helping another person in need.

After talking with Scott B., I regained some clarity and realized that drinking was the last thing I needed to do. I should've known by then that drugs and alcohol do not bring peace. Somehow, I had let myself drift away from a plan that had worked for me—a plan that had saved me from myself. I had not been faithfully working the last three steps: continuing to take a personal inventory and making immediate amends, praying and meditating regularly and consistently, and carrying this message to others. I knew that I needed to go to a meeting immediately, and reconnect with God and with service to others.

I started by praying right then and there. This prayer time was unlike the prayer and meditation I had been practicing for a long time. Over the years, my praying routine had dwindled to a quick gratuitous prayer when I happened to think about it. Christ was no longer guiding me and leading me. I had slipped back into pure self-will and self-reliance—the same behaviors that had contributed to my many problems early on. That was also the reason I had been feeling that hole in my heart growing and growing—I had been trying to fill a God-sized hole with money, prestige, and selfishness. This time I hit my knees and honestly asked God to come into my heart and my mind. I confessed my transgressions and asked Him to guide my thoughts and actions. I asked Him to replace my ego with His Holy Spirit. The relief and peace I felt was instantaneous. I didn't realize in that moment how far I had drifted from the source of power that had transformed my entire life.

I then went to a noon meeting to bolster my strength and renew my sense of purpose before I left for Mexico. At the meeting, I shared what had happened and what I'd been feeling in the last few months. Afterward, I went to lunch with several guys I'd met there. Everyone was very supportive and helped me understand that this kind of setback is to be expected when you stop doing the things that keep you sober and sane, and that I needed to renew my commitment to God and the twelve-step program. After sharing everything that was going on with Scott B. and the men from the meeting, I felt an immediate sense of relief. I knew what I needed to do, and I knew from my past experience that I could regain peace and serenity. I decided not to tell Becky about it until I returned from the trip, mainly because I didn't want her to worry the whole time I was out of town.

The next day, I went downtown to a halfway house where many of the men are homeless addicts and alcoholics, just like I was. A Better Way had closed down a number of years back, but this place was very similar. I showed up in time for the twelve fifteen meeting, and when I walked in, I saw a guy named John D. who had been at A Better Way with me in 1993. He had come in shortly before I left and we had quickly become friends. John D. is a couple years older than me, but the similarities in our addictions, our appearances, and our childhoods are startling. We are like two peas in a pod. However, I remained sober, while he had been in and out of the program, relapsing for the last fifteen years. He had just arrived at the halfway house the day before and was trying once again. Over the years, I had seen him at meetings every now and then, but inevitably he would disappear and I would lose track of him.

When we saw each other that day, we smiled and I went over and gave him a big hug. I asked him how he was doing and he replied, "Not so good." He shared with me that since he had gotten out of prison a year ago, he had been living in a cardboard box under a bridge downtown. He said that he had woken up the day before, soaked from the rain, and decided to give sobriety another try. I was glad to see John D. again, because he's one of the most likable guys I know. He's also one of the most intelligent, but for some reason he just won't commit himself to doing the work in the program. I asked him what had happened to him since A Better Way, and he gave me a quick rundown of what life had been like. In the fifteen years since we had been in treatment together, he had been in prison several times for a total of six years, lived on the street off and on for five years, killed a man with a knife in self-defense when he was attacked on the street, and held down a job and lived a somewhat normal life for about four years. It floored me when I heard what the last decade and a half had been like for him. I knew in my heart that I was no different than John D., and that his story could have been my story.

When the meeting was over, I told him that I really cared for him and that it was no accident I had come to that meeting. I asked if I could help him in some way. He requested that I sponsor him and take him through the steps, and I told him I would be honored to help. I instructed him to get started reading steps one, two, and three in the Big Book, and I made it clear that there was no way he could do this without the help of God. I made sure that he understood that he could decide on his own concept of God, but that he had to do so immediately, and then he needed to ask God for the strength to stay sober—one day at a time. I let him know that I would be going out of town for a few days, but that we would get together when I returned.

As I was driving home from the meeting and my visit with John D., I was suffused with a feeling of gratitude and peace. I knew that my purpose in life was to stay sober and help others transform their lives. Somehow, I had lost my way, but I was back on track, determined not to drink or use drugs in Mexico.

I felt fulfilled once again and my decision to stay sober wasn't rattled after I got to Mexico, even though Ziggy began partying almost the minute we got off the plane. We were picked up at the airport by Eduardo, a very wealthy Mexican man who had organized the concert. After we checked into our hotel and dropped off our things, he took us straight to a bar to see where the band's private party would be held that night. It was a huge bar that Eduardo owned, and the Dos Equis beer company was the sponsor for the party. Eduardo and Ziggy had a few beers at the bar, then we went to the hotel.

That night, we went with Eduardo to another restaurant/bar he owned. We had dinner with Thievery Corporation and a bunch of Eduardo's friends. Everyone was drinking and partying, and seemed to be enjoying themselves, but I wasn't tempted. I felt just as I had felt for the last fifteen years—I had absolutely no desire to drink or take drugs. I had come full circle and once again had no interest in drinking and getting high. Later that night as I watched everyone get drunk and crazy, I was grateful that I could hang out and have a good time without having to pay the consequences of getting sloppy drunk, losing control over my behavior, and suffering from a terrible hangover the next day. I woke up at nine o'clock the next morning feeling fresh and alive, and went exploring and shopping. That night, we went to the concert and had a blast watching the show from the VIP section on the side of the stage.

I was more convinced than ever that I wanted nothing to do with my old lifestyle. That behavior was in my past for good, provided I did what I needed to do. I knew in my heart that drugs and alcohol would never bring me the peace and joy I desired. Only God could give me the peace and fulfillment that I so deeply needed. It felt really good to be clear about who I was and what I stood for. I was grateful for the trip to Mexico; it reminded me how much I love the life I have in sobriety.

When I returned home, I immediately began scheduling regular twelve-step meetings and setting aside time for prayer and meditation. I also began looking into what I could do to mentor or counsel other recovering addicts or alcoholics. For me, true peace and joy is only found in helping others. All the money and possessions in the world cannot compare to the joy of helping another person to change his or her life for the better. The next day, I drove back down to the halfway house downtown and spent some time talking with John D. about steps one, two, and three. He had done the reading I asked, and we walked through his first three steps together. After we said the third-step prayer together, I instructed him to start working on his fourth step. I also spent some time there talking with other men, offering my time and support to them. I knew that they were no different than me; they were in the same position I had been in fifteen years ago, when I was living out of my truck.

Shortly after I came back from Mexico, I shared what had happened with Becky. At first, she was pretty upset that I had not told her earlier. However, once I explained that I needed the support of the men in the program to work through this, and that once I had worked through it I felt comfortable sharing it with her, she understood and supported me. She has always been the rock in my life, but some situations require the support of people who have firsthand experience. Within a few weeks, Becky said that the transformation I had undergone was amazing. She said it was like I had gone back to being the man she married, lighthearted, fun, and full of zest. Our connection and bond came alive again in a way it had not been for a long time.

My connection with our children also went to a new level. I was filled with love and peace from my renewed relationship with God, and from that place of fullness I was able to truly share that love. All of my external stress, combined with my inner turmoil, over the last several years had affected my relationship with my wife and children. During my time of crisis, I had been very self-absorbed and closed off emotionally. I became a "dry drunk," surviving on my own self-will, rather than turning that will over to God. I had regressed and had come dangerously close to using my old coping mechanisms—selfishness, self-centeredness, ego, control, and denial.

With my new sense of wholeness and purpose, I was able to connect with my family on a new level. Raising two children in diapers and handling the task of being a parent was difficult, but when my heart was closed, it felt like a burden. That's how I felt growing up and it terrified me to think that one of my children might grow up feeling the same way due to my actions. My children and my wife are the most precious gifts I have ever been entrusted with, and it is my honor and duty to love and serve them in the manner that God has served and loved me. Coming so close to the brink of destruction, and then coming out of it alive and unscathed, gave me a renewed sense of gratitude and appreciation for everything in my life. It scares me to even think about what might have happened to me if I had started drinking and drugging in Mexico.

It would have cost me my marriage and my family, and quite possibly my life.

Within a few months of finishing the transition period with my old company, I began giving a good deal of thought to what I would do next in my professional life, but every business idea that I pondered left something to be desired. My inability to get excited about any of these ideas had been intensely frustrating, and I was concerned about the uncertainty of my future. I had come to the conclusion that I had no desire to be retired at the age of thirty-five; I really enjoyed working and being a part of something. After that day at the treatment center, helping those men, I knew that I was supposed to help others, and that my new career would be in that vein.

I decided I would work with businesses from a different direction—I'd be a business coach. I knew firsthand what it took to make a business thrive and grow, and I also knew from my experience with Alistair how valuable the advice of an expert can be. I also immediately signed up to volunteer with a drug and alcohol treatment program at my church, which focused on teens and young adults, and I began volunteering at a crisis shelter for homeless youth. I've always enjoyed working with young people who are faced with similar challenges to those I experienced. I gain satisfaction from helping young people learn that no matter what hand they have been dealt, they can become who and what they want to be. In the early days of my sobriety, meeting people like me who had made it through and built a good life for themselves had been an important part of my recovery. I wanted to give that same inspiration to others.

Shortly after making this career decision, I spoke with my dad on the phone and shared with him that I had decided to do business coaching. He and I had gotten pretty close over the last five or six years, and we talked on the phone regularly. I told him that this would be a good way to help people and make a difference, while utilizing my experience and talent in business. My only concern was that I would only be able to work with twelve to fifteen companies at a time, and I had a desire to help many people, not just a few. My dad suggested that I consider writing a book to tell my story on a larger scale, and after some thought, I realized that writing a book and doing public speaking was the best way I could share my experience and hope with a wide audience. Without a doubt, I knew that this was the right plan for my life, and I felt entirely at peace. I knew deep in my heart that sharing my story to guide and inspire people, and using my life experience as a testament to God's grace and power, was exactly what God wanted me to do. Having this mission and purpose brought a feeling of peace to me that went all the way to my core. Without a higher purpose, life was dull and shallow, and I had no desire to go back to the life of being merely a consumer, or worse, an addict. With God's grace and support, and the assistance of my sponsor, friends, and family, I was living a transformed life, and I was never going back.

EPILOGUE

Writing a book…well that was a bold plan for me to undertake, but I'm the kind of person who likes a challenge, and I knew I could figure out how to do it. At a recent promotional event in Houston, the speaker James Arthur Ray said that successful people focus on resourcefulness, not resources. What he meant is that if we only look at what can be accomplished with the resources currently at our disposal, then we are most likely going to be severely limited. However, if we approach our goals with an attitude of resourcefulness, then we can accomplish them. Making the decision to write a book was the first step, and the easy part. The next step is where so many people have difficulty, and where most end their dreams and the opportunity to be successful. The next step is to take action and move forward with the decision. I had never written a book before, so I did not have the necessary resources at my disposal. So I exercised my resourcefulness. I began by doing research on the Internet and learned what it takes to write and publish a book. Then I got out the pen and paper and started writing.

The best place to start was at the beginning. I went back as far as I could remember and began writing any information or incident that seemed relevant. It was a little difficult to get going, but I just set aside a couple hours a day to write. What I didn't realize when I started the process was just how emotional it would be for me to revisit many of the experiences in my past. Overall, it has turned out to be a cleansing process for me. Many of those painful memories had been left alone since the time when I was in therapy over ten years ago, and revisiting them brought up some anger and resentment, which I was able to relieve myself of through prayer and discussion. All in all, it has been a great journey, both emotionally and spiritually.

It has also been good for Becky and me, because she learned a lot of things about my childhood that she didn't know. It's not that I intentionally withheld anything from Becky; it's just that I have not felt the need to discuss many of the incidents that occurred so long ago. Talking about my past brought us closer and deepened our bond. I was also worried that my family might be uncomfortable with me sharing information about their lives, so I made sure to talk with them before I was too far along in the process. I was relieved and happy that they wholeheartedly supported what I was doing. With a lot of time and work, my relationship with my parents has really come full circle. They have grown and matured just as I have. My father has even become a little more kind and affectionate in his golden years. My relationship with my mother is another wonderful gift in my life. She has been a great support mechanism for Becky and me, as well as our children. Having her around to help with the kids has given Becky and me the opportunity to spend a lot of time together and continue to grow closer. She has been an amazing grandmother to Mattox and Madison. I am truly grateful that I am able to have a good relationship with my parents.

I have continued to pursue my commitment to service by actively volunteering at a drug and alcohol treatment program at my church, and volunteering at a crisis shelter for homeless youth. The program at my church is called Teen and Family Services, and it's a Christian-based program that provides counseling and after-school activities for kids aged fourteen through eighteen. There is a heavy focus on peer group support, so the kids who are further along in the program help guide and support the newer kids. Teens listen to teens much more than they listen to adults. This follows in the tradition of the twelfth step in the Big Book, and Teen and Family also uses the twelve steps as a part of the program.

One of my roles in this program is to help facilitate an alumni meeting on Thursday nights. This meeting is a place where the graduates from the program can meet and talk about what is going on in their daily lives. As the facilitator, I try and offer my experience, strength, and hope in a way that can benefit them as they navigate the situations they are faced with. It's a pretty easy job, working with the alumni, because they have graduated from the program, and for the most part they are all staying sober and enjoying life. I was also honored with an invitation to be on the board of directors at Teen and Family Services, which I gladly accepted. To go from being a troubled teen to serving on the board of directors for a program that helps troubled teens turn their lives around is yet another testament to the power of God and the value of the twelve-step program. What an honor and a privilege it has been for me to be a part of these kids' lives and of a great organization like Teen and Family Services.

The other organization I have been volunteering at is Covenant House, a crisis shelter for homeless, runaway, and throwaway youth. If you're like me, you're probably wondering what a "throwaway youth" is. Unfortunately, many parents toss their children out on the street and leave them to fend for themselves. I guess that's similar to my story, except many of these kids don't get money for a hotel or an apartment. They end up homeless, living under a bridge. Covenant House offers food, shelter, clothing, medical attention, counseling, and long-term support for getting these kids stabilized and self-sufficient. It's an amazing organization that I get a lot out of. I love interacting with the kids and sharing my story to let them know that anything is possible. Many of these kids are facing the exact same challenges I faced when I was twenty and trying to turn my life around. It's important for them to know they can make it out of the situation they are in and they can be successful.

Spending my time serving at Teen and Family Services, as well as Covenant House, has been wonderfully fulfilling. I know my purpose is to use what has happened in my life to help inspire others to overcome their difficulties. I am also staying very active in the twelve-step program by going to meetings regularly, and sponsoring men who are trying to stay sober. I know grace is the only reason I made it through my close call with drinking, and I'm not going to waste my opportunity. Working the twelve steps, staying connected spiritually, and helping others is my recipe for success. I surely don't want to forget that again. There's too much on the line. I have the life I always dreamed of, and it would be crazy to throw it all away for a drink.

One of the main things I am trying to accomplish with this book is to educate and inspire people who have been directly or indirectly affected by the challenges I have faced. I hope that readers understand that this book is ultimately about finding a way to make it through life's challenges, not just dealing with addiction problems. Obviously, many people have not experienced the exact challenges I have faced, and I'm sure that there are many solutions other than the ones I have used. In the end, what's important to me is that this book gives people the inspiration to seek the truth, find their solutions, take action, and live a good and full life.

Throughout this book I have been as honest as possible and have tried to share with you the challenges that have shaped my life. These next few pages are written in that spirit of honesty. I've talked a lot about me and the principles that I employed in this journey to success. Drawing on my experiences, I would like to offer you, the reader, observations I have made in my growth that I hope you will benefit from.

How does one transition from despair to hope in this life? How does one go from being homeless and living in a truck to being retired at thirty-five and living in a nice home with an amazing wife and two beautiful children? How can that be possible? You may not think it's possible, but as I have recounted with my story, I am living proof it is. I lived in that truck with a Hefty bag containing all my worldly possessions. I was alone, filthy, and ashamed, wondering daily where I would eventually take a shower. I was plagued with seemingly insurmountable cravings that caused me to fear for my freedom and life. Now I am a whole man in mind, body, and spirit who no longer fears life, but embraces it to the fullest.

For every addict who sobers up, only one in a hundred stays that way. I am that one in a hundred (by God's grace), and so far I have been able to achieve it in the same way that millions of others before me have achieved it—through spirituality and faith. Only by allowing God to come into my life could I make the transformation from where I started to where I am now. The past does not equal the future for me because I turned my life and will over to something greater than myself. For me, that something greater started out as God and naturally evolved into Jesus Christ.

Every time I have connected to Christ and allowed Him to be the Lord of my life, miracles have occurred. In fact, I think this is a book of miracles. It is very important for me to acknowledge that, for me, this power of transformation comes from Him. The principles and thoughts I discuss below have been pivotal in my own journey of grace, and I believe they will have the same effect on everyone who utilizes them. May God bless you on your journey of miracles.

So what's next? Well, I am excited to tell my story with the hope of inspiring others to take action and overcome their difficulties, but the next step is to really define and put into words the specific details and the actions I took to make it through the various problems I faced. As my book neared completion, I worked to identify and put into words the actions and principles that I learned and implemented to overcome my challenges, and to achieve my goals. This list is a work in progress, and I plan on writing another book that will further define and describe in greater detail these things. For now, I'll share the ones that I feel are crucial to being successful in any area of life—be it physical, relational, spiritual, or financial. These principles can be applied to all areas of life. I hope that the following thoughts and ideas are helpful and make a difference for you.

Honesty

Without the ability to be honest with ourselves about our emotions, spiritual condition, relationships, health, finances, careers, or any other part of our lives, there is no possibility of change. If we are not willing to honestly acknowledge that an area or several areas of our lives are not what we want them to be, then we will not be able to start the process of change and healing. Denial, rationalization, and justification are the tools we use to keep from having to really take a good look at our lives and face them for what they are. Obviously, if we do not acknowledge there is a problem, then we will never seek or find a solution.

I lived in denial about my alcoholism and addiction for many years in order to keep from having to face it. I found every way possible to justify and rationalize my behavior, because if I really looked at what I was doing, then I might actually have to do something about my situation. Since I had no idea what solutions were available to me, the thought of changing seemed impossible. Once I found out that there was a solution, I had hope. My hope came from people in the program who had been put in my life by God, and had gone down the path I had gone down and were successful in overcoming their problems.

I have developed this ability to be honest with myself and seek solutions over many years (it isn't easy), and I have applied this principle in nearly every part of my life. Whenever I am dissatisfied with a situation, I take an honest inventory of myself—first to understand the problem and then to secure a solution.

In every case, both the problem and the solution are within me. That's not to say that I don't need outside help to solve my problems. However, I have continually had to accept that my actions, reactions, and choices are the root of my problems, and can also be the solutions. Changing the way I act, and changing the choices I make, are the keys to changing the results I get from any area of my life. Once I was willing to accept that I was the key factor in all my problems, and that I had the ability and power to change the situation, then and only then was I ready to change.

The question is how do we get honest with ourselves? An easy answer is to ask ourselves if we are truly satisfied with the results we are getting in the various areas of our lives. If we can answer yes to every area of our lives, then I would say we are still not being honest. If I met someone who told me every aspect of his life was perfect, then I would question his honesty. Nobody is perfect, and introspection is a lifelong process. It's important to realize that honestly looking within and finding out that something is not the way we want it, is not a negative. It's ultimately a positive if we choose to address the situation, because then we have the opportunity to change and find more peace and satisfaction.

Open-mindedness

In order for change to occur, I have to have an open mind, not only to the possibility of change, but, many times, to the resources available to help me change. When I was finally ready to acknowledge my drug and alcohol problem, I had to be open to the solution available in the twelve-step program.

This attitude of open-mindedness gives us the opportunity to look beyond our own set of abilities, and find new help and support to navigate through the situation we are faced with. It only seems logical that if I could solve my problems with the knowledge and ability I *already* possessed, then I would have solved my problems on my own long before my life became a complete shambles. Humility is a requirement to be able to reach out for help because in it we acknowledge that we do not have all of the answers. Humility can also be described as "teachable." When I am teachable and have an open mind, then I am in a place where change is really possible. It is important to not only be open to the various solutions others have used to be successful in any given situation, but also to actually accept and contemplate the advice and guidance these people offer.

One of the most difficult yet rewarding things that I had to be open-minded about was the idea that there is a God, and that a relationship with God could help me overcome my issues. This one was by far the hardest concept for me to digest, and it has proven to be the most powerful. It seems that in life, the greatest rewards come from the most challenging situations. Marriage, family, business, and faith have been my biggest challenges, but they have also been the source of my greatest rewards.

Action

When I say "action," what I mean is work, work, and more work. The only way I have ever been successful at anything I have attempted is by hard work and diligence. When I entered the twelve-step program, I was informed that it was a spiritual program of action. This meant that God was there to give me strength, but that *I* had to do the work to recover. God loved me too much to leave me stuck, and all I had to do was seek Him and let Him into my life. Once I did this, He was able to do amazing things in me. I've said many times that God can move mountains, but you better bring your shovel. Another one of my favorite sayings is "Pray like it depends on God, and work like it depends on you."

Focused energy and action is what is required to be successful. If you watch great athletes, you can see their intensity and focus when they are at the top of their game. It's as if time stands still for them. An example of focused energy is the difference between a light bulb that puts off enough soft light to light a room, and a laser that uses the same energy to cut through a piece of steel. When we focus our energy and effort, we can accomplish the most difficult of tasks. Action or energy with no focus will not get the job done. People who confuse the two are always frantically busy, yet never seem to get anything done.

I had to focus on working the twelve steps and put in the time before I got the rewards. In my business life, I had to intensely focus my energy, work long hours, and struggle through hard times before I received the financial rewards. My marriage has required constant focus and work to stay healthy, and continue to improve and grow. The work and action required to raise my children the way I would have liked to have been raised is the pinnacle of this principle. The list goes on and on.

I have not found any shortcuts in life and it's not from a lack of searching. Our society wants to tell us that we can take a pill to be happy, or spend four minutes a month exercising on some special machine and then everything will be perfect, and we will be healthy and happy and gorgeous. To that I say with sincerity, "Yeah, right!"

I can only speak from experience, and my experience has taught me that anything lasting requires effort. It has taken a long time for me to learn to embrace this concept, but after realizing and accepting that hard work is the key to success, I quit fretting and moved into action. However, my actions were pointless without faith. If you don't believe that your hard work will pay off, then it's going to be nearly impossible to be motivated. I strengthened my faith by looking at what people I respected had done to be successful. I knew that if they could do it, then there's no reason I couldn't do it as well. Over time, after experiencing some of the rewards of hard work for myself, I was able to use my own experience as motivation to keep putting in the effort to achieve my goals.

People

Without the help and support of other people, I could never have done the things I have been able to do in my life. The idea that we can be successful at anything without help is absurd. After all, even the Lone Ranger had Tonto. My wife, family, friends, therapists, business coach, employers, employees, and many others, have helped me in every area of my life. It has been critical for me to seek out and utilize the support available to me.

Our ego wants to tell us that we can do it without help, which keeps us stuck in the situation we are in. My ego almost stopped me from hiring my business coach, Alistair, who was a huge help in building our landscape business. After working with him, I came to understand that the reason someone as great as Tiger Woods uses a coach is not only to become better, but also because *he can't see himself* swinging the club with the same clarity that an observer can. It's the same for all of us in some form or fashion. We need people who can help us to see what we cannot see ourselves. Either we cannot see something because we are in the middle of it, or we can't see something because of a lack of knowledge and understanding. Alistair helped me because he had more knowledge and experience in areas I was lacking in. He also showed me things I'd overlooked because I was in the middle of the situation.

I have a person that I coach in business who owns a chain of pharmacies. In some of our early sessions, he began to get frustrated with himself because he had never done or seen some of the things I was showing him. My response was to ask him why he thought he should already have known the things we were discussing. He was trained and schooled to be a pharmacist, not an entrepreneur—why should he possess all of the knowledge and skills needed to run a business? The important thing was to find a way to get the knowledge, skills, and support necessary to get where he wanted to go in his business. That was the reason he and I were meeting.

I also believe that it's critical to surround yourself with people who are on the same path in life that you are. This fellowship with others helps to give us motivation and support to stay on the path and stay focused. It's important to not only surround yourself with people on the same path, but you must surround yourself with the *successful* people on that path. Only people who are more successful or further along in the journey can show you how to get where they are. If I want to grow a business, and then sell that business, I need to connect with someone who has already accomplished that in order to learn how it's done. I'm surely not going to go ask a bachelor, or someone thrice divorced, for advice on marriage.

A perfect example of utilizing the power of people is the time I spend in fellowship with successful participants of the twelve-step program. We give each other support and strength to stay on the path of sobriety and recovery. There are organizations where you can get support for practically every facet of life. Whether it's business, faith, recovery, or weight loss, you name it and there are groups or organizations where people are supporting each other to achieve a common goal.

Service

Service is the cornerstone to true fulfillment. When I sold my company and had the "success" defined by today's society, I still felt empty and unfulfilled, primarily due to a lack of serving others. I had free time, plenty of money, a nice house, a new car, a great wife, wonderful kids, great friends, good health—you name it and I had it. Many people probably will have a hard time understanding how I could have felt unfulfilled when everything seemed so ideal in my life. Don't get me wrong; I enjoyed and appreciated all of those things. However, for me, the fact of the matter is that without the internal fulfillment of connecting with other people, and serving their needs unselfishly, no amount of "stuff" will ever provide true lasting peace and joy. Internalizing this critical concept, and then acting on it, is crucial to lifelong fulfillment.

When I am focused on helping someone else, I am living in the moment and all of the fear, guilt, sadness, and anxiety of yesterday and tomorrow vanishes. In the process of helping someone else, I'm able to stop worrying about me, and focus on another's needs. This is a liberating sensation that allows me to connect at a spiritual level, and to leave my worldly issues behind.

No matter who you are, or how much you have, you will be faced with difficult times in life when your external world is not where you want it. It may be money, health, relationships, or any number of issues that we all face at some time or another. If we are not capable of finding fulfillment at the spiritual level, then we will be victims of the external circumstances outside of our control. We will inevitably give control of our emotional lives over to circumstance.

It doesn't have to be a complex process to find someone or somewhere to serve. Coworkers, friends, family, churches, neighbors, and community programs can all be great people and places to serve. If we keep our eyes and hearts open, we will perceive need. In the twelve-step program, we have a saying: "You have to give it away to keep it." Giving love and support to others is the way to have it for yourself. Christ served, and by serving He lead and people followed.

Pastor Jim at Chapelwood closes every sermon with the following prayer, and even after twelve years of hearing it I still get moved every time he says it. I would like to share this prayer with you in closing.

May the Lord bless you and keep you. May the Lord make His face to shine upon you, and be gracious unto you. May the Lord lift the light of His countenance upon you and give you peace, both now and always, in the name of the Father, the Son, and the Holy Spirit. Amen.

RESOURCES

Al-Anon and Alateen (Support for the loved ones of alcoholics and addicts.)
http://www.alanon.org

Alcoholics Anonymous
http://www.aa.org

American Association of Christian Counselors
http://www.aacc.net

Cocaine Anonymous
http://www.ca.org

Licensed Therapists/Counselors
http://www.ecounseling.com
http://www.findcounseling.com

Narcotics Anonymous
http://www.na.org